AGNES MARSHALL:
FROM SCULLERY MAID TO VICTORIAN CELEBRITY COOK

Agnes Marshall:

From Scullery Maid to Victorian Celebrity Cook

DAVID SMITH

Agnes Marshall: From Scullery Maid to Victorian Celebrity Cook

© David W. Smith, 2023 – revised edition

Imprint: KDP

ISBN 9798866395224

The right of David W. Smith to be identified as the author of this work has been asserted by him in accordance with the Copyright, Designs and Patents Act 1988.

A CIP catalogue record for this book is available from the British Library.

All rights reserved. No part of this book may be reproduced, stored in a retrieval system, or transmitted by any other means, electronic, mechanical, photocopying, recording or otherwise, without the express prior permission of the author. This book may not be lent, resold, hired out or otherwise disposed of by way of trade in any form of binding or cover other than that in which it is published, without the prior consent of the author.

Contents

Preface	7
From Scullery Maid to Entrepreneur	9
Table Talk	25
Brilliant Lectures and a Cookery Book	41
Company Business	51
Exhibitions	63
Family Matters	77
Memorials and Myths	87
Class and Social Mobility	98
Was Mrs Marshall the new Mrs Beeton?	104
Ice and Ice Cream	110
The Servant Question	122
Online Pictures	133
Publication Dates for Agnes Marshall's Books	134
Primary Sources	140
Further Reading	141
Notes	142
Index	162

Preface

After I had published my previous book, *The Cooking Colonel of Madras*, I was looking for a new project. Agnes Marshall had made a brief appearance in the book – the advertisements for her cookery school had appeared alongside Colonel Kenney-Herbert's in the London daily newspapers. I had never heard of Mrs A. B. Marshall before then, but she sounded like an interesting character. The more I found out about her life and achievements, the more fascinating she became.

The writer and celebrity cook Fanny Craddock was a great admirer of Agnes Marshall's work and had intended to write a biography of her with the title: *The Great Marshall Mystery*. Unfortunately, it was never published although the recipes in Craddock's work, *The Sherlock Holmes Cookbook*, were largely taken from Agnes's cookery books.

As far as I am aware, Agnes Marshall left no diaries or other personal memoirs. A major work on her life and accomplishments was published in 1998 with the title *Mrs Marshall: The Greatest Victorian Ice Cream Maker*. The book is the work of several contributors – Robin Weir, John Deith, Peter Brears and Peter Barham – whose essays were originally presented to the Oxford Symposium on Food and Cookery in 1995. The book has been an invaluable source of information in my research. However, Deith seems to have gained much of his information about Agnes's personal life by interviewing members of the Marshall family. As is often the case with family folklore, some of their recollections have proven to be a little unreliable. I have made use of recent research and conducted my own to piece together the most likely story of Agnes's early years (which is considerably different from what was previously thought).

Agnes and her husband Alfred started to publish a weekly newspaper on food and dining in 1886. The paper was called *The Table* and continued to be published until long after Agnes's death. I have spent many long hours in the British Library reading all editions of the paper covering sixteen years. A great deal of information in this book comes from *The Table*, but much of its content was dedicated to society gossip and social trivia. While such topics are historically interesting, they provide little insight into Agnes or her business affairs, so I have skipped over them wherever possible.

I would like to thank the staff of the British Library and The National Archives for their assistance in helping me to find the references I needed. A new resource for me, the London Metropolitan Archives, proved invaluable in providing evidence that had previously lacked verifiable sources. I would especially like to thank Louise Harrison for finding the material I needed. I had the easiest visit possible because she arranged for the records to be ready and waiting for me the moment I arrived.

Special thanks are due to my editor, Michelle Higgs. Not only is she a thoughtful and diligent editor, but she is also an accomplished author in her own right. Her extensive knowledge of Victorian society was invaluable in making sure that I had correctly understood the social factors which influenced Agnes Marshall's life.

Finally, I could not have completed this book without the support of my wife, Kathy Slack OBE. I am hugely grateful to her for keeping me on track when, inevitably, the writing did not go as smoothly as I would have liked.

David Smith
Oxfordshire, June 2023

From Scullery Maid to Entrepreneur

The performance ended with the audience applauding enthusiastically. What they had just witnessed was not a play or a concert but a cookery demonstration. Agnes Bertha Marshall had displayed to almost 600 people how to prepare and cook "A Pretty Luncheon" in the prestigious surroundings of Willis's Rooms in London. After the luncheon had been prepared, the audience were invited up to the stage to inspect the finished dishes which "attracted much admiration" according to *The Morning Post* of 17 October 1887, two days later.[1] *The Times* reviewed the event in glowing terms, reporting that Marshall had "completely engrossed the earnest attention" of those who watched her performance. The fact that Agnes Marshall still featured extracts from the newspaper reviews in her cookery books some eighteen years later indicates how proud she must have felt about her accomplishment that day.[2]

Agnes Marshall is a fascinating example of Victorian social mobility. From humble origins, she became the toast of the contemporary culinary scene with her name above the door of her own cookery school and as the author of a cookery book endorsed by royalty.

John Deith, in the seminal book on Agnes Marshall's life, *Mrs Marshall: The Greatest Victorian Ice Cream Maker*,[3] tells us that she was born Agnes Bertha Smith on 24 August 1855 in Walthamstow.[4] Her parents were John and Susan Smith. Agnes's future marriage certificate records that John Smith's occupation was a clerk.

The birth records from 1855 do not provide clear evidence for Agnes's birth. This lack of information has given rise to uncertainties about Agnes's early life. Some researchers have concluded that her history is quite different from the generally accepted version related above. An essay by Terry Jenkins, published in the journal *Petits Propos Culinaires*, claims that Agnes was born in 1852, not 1855; that Susan Smith was a single mother; and that John Smith was invented some years later by Agnes to give the impression that she was the daughter of a clerk to whom her mother was married at the time of her birth.[5]

The lack of evidence from the official records does not necessarily mean that Agnes was not born in 1855. It could be that the records have been transcribed incorrectly or are missing altogether. Significantly, the theory that she was born in 1852 is at odds with the age she stated on the census returns,[6] and the age her family declared her to be on her death certificate and memorial window in Pinner Parish Church.[7]

However, the suggestion that Agnes was born to a single mother does seem to be correct. Agnes's mother, Susan Smith, married a man named John Wells in April 1869. Wells was a cabinetmaker from St Neots in Huntingdonshire. He is recorded in the 1861 census as staying with his brother Charles, also a cabinetmaker, in Brunswick Street, Shoreditch,[8] along with Charles's wife and four children.[9] Susan Smith declares herself on their marriage certificate to be a "spinster" rather than a widow (as she would have been if she had previously been married to a John Smith who had subsequently died). She states that she is the daughter of Joseph Smith, a carpenter.[10] Susan's declaration gives considerable weight to the suggestion that Agnes did not have a father named John Smith who was a clerk.

If Agnes was not averse to manipulating the facts about her parentage, it may be that she was also economical with the truth regarding her age. On balance, the evidence suggests that Jenkins is correct when he claims that she was born Agnes Beere Smith in 1852 and that she changed her middle name to Bertha at some later date.[11] I discuss his research concerning Agnes's early years in the chapter: Memorials and Myths.

Susan Smith and John Wells had three children before they were married. The children's birth records indicate that their last name was registered as Smith, but that they each had an additional first name of Wells. Mary Sarah Wells Smith was born in 1859, John Osborn Wells Smith in 1863 and Ada Martha W[ells] Smith in 1868. Mary, John and Ada were therefore Agnes's half-siblings.

At the time of the 1871 census, John and Susan Wells were living at 41 Princes Street, Shoreditch, along with Mary, John and Ada. Agnes is not living with her mother and stepfather on the night of the census; if Jenkins is right, she would have been eighteen. Whether she had left home or whether she was merely absent that day is unknown – the record only states who was staying where on census night. The most likely scenario is that Agnes had already started on her career path, and was working as a cook's assistant, known as a scullery maid. If that was the case, she would have been living at her employer's residence.

41 Princes Street was in the parish of St Leonards.[12] Two families shared the house – five members of the Wells family and five of a family named Newby. According to Charles Booth's *Maps Descriptive of London Poverty*,[13] Princes Street was occupied by households who were "Fairly comfortable. Good ordinary earnings", the same class of income that John Wells and his brother enjoyed when they lived in Brunswick Street ten years earlier.

The first time that Agnes Bertha Smith appears in the official records is when she married Alfred William Marshall on 17 August 1878. Both were stated to be of "full" age, which meant over the age of twenty-one; in fact, Alfred was almost thirty-one and Agnes was twenty-five (although she would have claimed to be twenty-two). The marriage took place at the parish church of St George, Hanover Square.[14] Alfred Marshall gives his profession as a merchant whose father, Thomas, was a builder. Agnes is not recorded as having a profession although she would have been working as a cook for some years previously. Alfred gives us a brief glimpse of Agnes's early career in an interview with the *Pall Mall Gazette*, published in October 1886, in which he says "Mrs. Marshall, I should tell you, has made a thorough study of cookery ever since she was a child, and has practised at Paris and Vienna under celebrated chefs."[15] If that is true, and not just Alfred talking up Agnes's credentials, she would have worked abroad in her early twenties. A passport was issued on 15 August 1874 in the name of Miss A. B. Smith according to the Register of Passport Applications, but whether this is indeed Agnes or merely a namesake, we do not know. Agnes later wrote that her recipes were "the result of practical training and lessons, through several years, from leading English and Continental authorities, as well as a home experience earlier than I can well recall".[16]

Alfred's family history is better documented than Agnes's. He was born in Taplow, Buckinghamshire, on 21 August 1847. His father had died by the time of the 1851 census when Alfred was three years old and his younger sister, Eliza, was only one. Living with Alfred's mother and her children were two lodgers, plasterers who had presumably worked for Alfred's father in his construction business. Sadly, tragedy was soon to strike once again: by the time Alfred was thirteen, his mother had also died, and Alfred had become a resident at the British Orphan Asylum in Clapham. The orphanage outgrew its premises in Clapham and moved to new premises in Slough, Berkshire, in 1863.[17] Although circumstances were desperate for the young Alfred, he seems to have been intelligent and was educated well by the orphanage's teachers. He became a teacher himself – the census of 1871 shows Alfred to be an assistant master at Oakley House Gentleman's School in Reading, Berkshire. As we have seen, at the time of his marriage seven years later, Alfred had sidelined his teaching career to become a merchant. To be more specific, he identifies himself as a wine merchant on his daughter's birth certificate in 1879.

The next phase in the lives of the newly married Mr and Mrs Marshall must have caused great anxiety and distress for them both. Alfred was sentenced at the Old Bailey on 31 March 1879 to six months' imprisonment for the embezzlement of nearly £275.[18] He had entered into a partnership with a man named William Houghton and a wine merchant from Xeres (Jerez) in Spain, Edwin Adolphus Ross Crusoe. The three men were thinking big. Their arrangement was for Crusoe to supply £3,000 worth of wine, and for Marshall and Houghton to provide £2,000 capital for carrying on the business in England. That is about £295,000 and £197,000 respectively in today's money.[19] The likelihood of Alfred and Houghton providing the necessary capital seems hopelessly optimistic and indeed may have been a fraudulent claim. Matters started to go wrong early in the partnership. Crusoe made two shipments of wine and the barrels were stored in a bonded warehouse, but payments on account made to Crusoe by Marshall & Houghton had not been honoured by their bank. Houghton vanished and re-emerged in South Africa. Alfred then persuaded the Dowgate Bonded Warehouse to advance him £275 on the understanding that he owned the wine in the warehouse. At that point, Crusoe worked out what was happening and had Alfred arrested. Alfred was found guilty but was "recommended to mercy by the jury on account of his youth" (even though he was thirty-one at the time) and because of the lax arrangements made by Crusoe at the bonded warehouse.[20]

The transcript of the trial reveals some details about Agnes and Alfred's life. Crusoe had visited Alfred at his home in November 1878 and recalls that he met Agnes there. He describes the property, 23 Royal Crescent, Notting Hill, as "a good house well furnished". The property was rented by Alfred from 19 August 1878 until the time of his committal. This means that he and Agnes moved into the house two days after their wedding. Where Agnes lived after Alfred was sent to prison is unknown, but she was already pregnant with their daughter, Agnes Alfreda, at the time. The baby girl was born a few weeks after Alfred was released from prison. Alfred did not describe himself to his landlord as a wine merchant, but as "one of the head assistants at the Stationers' School", so it appears that he had two distinct occupations running in parallel.[21]

According to John Deith, Agnes and Alfred had four children: "Ethel, born in 1879, Agnes, known as Aggie in the family, also in 1879, Alfred in 1880 and William born in 1882".[22] Deith interviewed members of the Marshall family for a paper he wrote for the Oxford Symposium on Food and Cookery in 1995 (which subsequently became chapter II in *Mrs Marshall: The Greatest Victorian Ice Cream Maker*), and he appears to have gained much of his information about Agnes's children from those conversations. However, Deith's claim that Ethel was born in 1879 is almost certainly not accurate, although it does pose some interesting questions.

The records at the General Register Office (GRO) show that only one Ethel Marshall was born to a mother with the maiden name of Smith in 1879 (there were none in 1878). That particular child was born in Stoke-on-Trent and her parents were Levi and Catherine Marshall, so that is not the Ethel Marshall we are looking for. It may be that Ethel was a nickname or a middle name which became permanent, or that she was born with an entirely different forename. What is certain is that Ethel was conceived before Agnes and Alfred were married. The birth certificate of their second child, Agnes Alfreda (a clever combination of their own names), shows that she was born on 16 October 1879 in Chelsea. It was highly unusual for premature babies to survive in Victorian times so Agnes Alfreda would have been conceived in late January 1879. If Ethel **was** born in 1879 as Deith claims, there must have been an incredibly short period between her birth and Agnes Alfreda's conception. If that is the case, Agnes would have been about five months pregnant with Ethel when she married Alfred. However, there is no child named Ethel, and no other female children apart from Agnes Alfreda, living with Agnes and Alfred at the time of the census of 1881.

The evidence suggests that Ethel was born **before** Agnes married Alfred and that she was born in 1878 as Ethel Smith. The 1881 census, taken on the night of 3 April, shows an Ethel Smith living with Agnes's mother and stepfather, and she is described as a grandchild. The record indicates that she was two years old which, if correct, implies that she was born between April 1878 and March 1879. The circumstances surrounding Ethel's birth are discussed further in the chapter: Memorials and Myths. If we jump forward ten years to the 1891 census taken on the night of 5 April, we find Ethel Marshall and Agnes Alfreda Marshall living at a boarding school in Arundel Terrace, Brighton. Ethel is twelve and Agnes Alfreda is eleven.

While such matters raise no concerns these days, in Victorian times it would have been socially disastrous to become a single mother if you were an ambitious young woman who was keen to climb the social ladder. In an article for the British Library, Ruth Richardson explains, "To become pregnant before being married was regarded as a source of shame for a woman in the early Victorian era [...] The stigma did not apply to unmarried fathers."[23] In practical terms, Agnes would have had to leave her job before Ethel was born. Employers did not want the burden of having servants with "encumbrances" (namely: children). Agnes would have found herself a new position in domestic service after the birth, and left baby Ethel to be cared for by her grandmother. Quite how Agnes and Alfred explained the circumstances of Ethel's birth we do not know, but by the time of the 1891 census she was firmly established as a member of the Marshall family.

The GRO records show that Alfred Harold Marshall was born in the first quarter of 1881[24] and that William Edward Marshall was born in the second quarter of 1882. Agnes had no more children. From now on, she would devote her attention to her career as a cookery instructor.

After the trauma of his time in prison, Alfred returned to being a private tutor. His work must have been quite lucrative – the 1881 census shows that Alfred and Agnes were living at 6 Wellington Road, near Lord's Cricket Ground, in the upmarket neighbourhood of St. John's Wood.[25] Charles Booth's maps confirm that Alfred and Agnes were comfortably off – Wellington Road is classed as being "Middle class. Well-to-do." Agnes was going up in the world.

Agnes Marshall did not wait long to launch her cookery school. Her first advertisements appear in the London daily newspapers in June 1883. The business is described as "A. B. Marshall (late Lavenue) School of Cookery" with premises at 67 Mortimer Street, London, and described as "established 1857".[26] What the advertisement means, of course, is that the Lavenue School of Cookery was established in 1857, not Marshall's, but it gives the fledgling business a reassuringly established air.[27] At some point in the autumn of 1883 Agnes Marshall moved her cookery school from 67 Mortimer Street to 30 Mortimer Street, where it would remain for the rest of its existence.[28] Alfred Marshall explained the reason for the move in his interview with the *Pall Mall Gazette*:

> It is now three years since we bought a house across the road in which a so-called school of cookery was carried on. Virtually, however, we had to start quite afresh; and after much thought as to whether a venture of this kind would have any chance of success, we acquired part of our present premises, had everything arranged and fitted up so as to suit our purpose, and announced publicly that Mrs. Marshall would on a certain date give lessons in practical cookery.[29]

It is intriguing to speculate how the Marshalls raised the capital to buy an existing cookery school and its premises, but Alfred is not forthcoming in the interview. It is possible that he had put aside some money gained from his dubious dealings as a wine merchant. If that is true, he clearly would not want the information known to a newspaper now that he and Agnes were established business proprietors, and the scandal of his conviction was conveniently forgotten.

The cookery school was slow to attract business at first. Alfred recalls the early days to the reporter of the *Pall Mall Gazette*:

> Well, on the day appointed for opening our school, everything was in working order, the grate, kitchen utensils, and all the various ingredients were ready, but no pupils arrived, and you can imagine that it was a loss to us, as fish and many other things would not keep longer than a day. On the second day it was the same, and for several days there seemed to be no prospect for us. But we continued our efforts by advertising and trying to make our plans as widely known as possible, and by-and-by pupils began to drop in, first one by one, then perhaps two, three, and up to half a dozen. The longer we went on the more our system was appreciated.[30]

The advertisements that Alfred talks about pepper the London daily newspapers, particularly *The Morning Post* and *The Evening Standard*. Within a year, the school's advertisements were able to boast of rave reviews in many respected journals and regional newspapers: "excellent classes", "cleverly imparted instruction", "genius for cookery" and similar high praise was heaped upon the school.[31] By mid-1884, the cookery school had changed its name from A. B. Marshall School of Cookery to Marshall's School of Cookery.[32]

Marshall's School of Cookery was not solely a cookery school. Like the Lavenue School of Cookery before it, Marshall's was set up to include "a special department for the engagement of cooks only" – in other words, an employment agency for cooks and, later, other domestic staff. Alfred explains how the agency came into being in his interview with the *Pall Mall Gazette*:

> As to our registry of cooks, we began it merely because ladies who had heard about our school came very often to see whether we could not get them a good cook from among our pupils. During the two years since we first opened it some 6,500 ladies have applied for cooks, while only 3,700 cooks have applied for situations. Pupils are registered free of charge, other cooks pay a fee of a shilling; but this is merely a safeguard against all kinds of women who come and offer themselves as cooks. Cooks known to have a doubtful character are rigorously excluded from the registry. On an engagement being concluded, both cooks and ladies pay us a certain engagement fee […][33]

Alfred goes on to lament that he had no trouble with the cooks paying their engagement fees, but the employers were often slow in paying or did not pay at all – that is, until the next time they required a cook when he would courteously remind them that their account was overdue. He estimated that the school lost around £200 per year from the non-payment of fees. Marshall's was casting its net wide to attract suitable applicants as cooks. In the autumn of 1885, it placed regular advertisements in regional newspapers – including those in Yorkshire, South Wales, Manchester, Sheffield and Bristol – inviting applicants to send for a prospectus for vacancies as cooks.

Agnes was gaining a growing reputation as a cookery teacher, but she was beginning to focus on the culinary topic for which she is best remembered: ice cream. She was clearly dissatisfied with the quality of the existing equipment for making and storing ice cream because she invented a more efficient design for a "freezing machine" and an "ice cave". Some modern writers have incorrectly claimed that it was Agnes who patented the design of the machines.[34] In fact, it was Alfred who applied for the patents for both machines and to whom they were granted in November 1884 and June 1885 respectively. Women were certainly entitled to apply for patents at that time[35] so it is puzzling why Agnes chose not to do so. It could well be that Alfred designed the machines according to Agnes's specifications, and therefore made the patent application himself. He confidently describes the freezing machine in the patent application as being "my design" and "my invention". Incidentally, Alfred declares himself to be a tutor for the purposes of the application, so he had not yet abandoned his teaching career.

Robin Weir tells us that the earliest ice cream machine was invented and patented in 1843 by Nancy Johnson in the USA, closely followed a year later by a machine patented by Thomas Masters in England.[36] Marshall's design was intended to improve upon that of existing machines. Marshall's machine, known as the "Patent Freezer", was primarily intended for domestic use, and the improvements were designed to save time and effort as well as reducing the amount of ice and salt needed for the freezing process. The design was wider and shallower than existing machines; instead of the tub containing the ice cream being surrounded by the ice and salt mixture, it was entirely cooled from below. The benefit of Marshall's design was the ease with which it could be assembled, used to make ice cream and cleaned afterwards.

The outer tub of the machine was made of wooden slats held tightly together by two metal hoops, resembling half a wine barrel. A central spindle or "pivot" was fixed to the bottom of the tub. Crushed ice was poured into the bottom and coarse salt was mixed into the ice. A metal freezing pan with a hollow central shaft was then located on the spindle and lowered into the tub until its base made contact with the ice and salt mixture. The amount of ice in the bottom of the tub could be varied depending on the volume of ice cream being made – there was sufficient clearance at the top of the tub to accommodate various heights for the freezing pan. A loose-fitting lid was placed on top of the freezing pan. There was a small "door" in the lid through which the cream mixture was poured, and which could be opened to check on the progress of the freezing process. Once the lid was in place, a turning handle was screwed onto the central shaft. The freezing pan had two opposing paddles or "fans" attached to the shaft. Unlike modern ice cream-making machines where the paddles rotate to mix the ice cream, the fans in Marshall's Patent Freezer were stationary, and it was the freezing pan that rotated when the handle was turned.

Marshall's advertisements featured a cross-section of the freezing machine with the caption: "Showing the fan inside, which remains still while the pan revolves and scrapes up the film of ice [cream] as it forms on the bottom of the pan".[37] The machine could be dismantled after use to clean the component parts, and a bung could be opened in the outer tub to release the melted, salty ice.

Marshall's claimed that ice cream could be made in the Patent Freezer in as little as three minutes, which is quite an achievement. Its newspaper advertisements boasted that the machine had received "three highest awards in 1885" – at the International Inventions Exhibition, the Exposition Culinaire Internationale and the International Food and Cookery Exhibition.[38] The design was protected "by Royal Letters Patent" and was patented in "all leading countries". The freezer was available in different sizes – the four most popular being able to freeze up to one, two, four or six quarts of ice cream.[39] Marshall's could supply larger sizes on request.

The patent for "Improvements in 'Ice Caves'" was submitted in September 1884, but was not granted until June 1885. An ice cave is described in the patent application as an "apparatus for freezing soufflés and moulding ice puddings and the like" – in other words, the Victorian equivalent of a modern electric freezer. At the time, the usual method of freezing moulded desserts was to place a lid onto the mould and seal the lid to the mould with grease. The mould was then lowered into a bucket containing ice and salt. A significant drawback of the process was that the seal might break, with the result that grease from the seal and salt from the ice mixture would contaminate the dessert.

Marshall's Ice Cave dispensed with sealed moulds by placing an open mould directly onto a shelf within the Ice Cave which had two doors. The one at the top allowed an inner container to be slotted inside the insulated outer container with the void between the two being filled with an ice and salt mixture. The void at the front of the Ice Cave was sealed so that no ice mixture could escape when the front door was opened. The front door itself was filled from the top with ice and salt so that the interior of the Ice Cave was surrounded by the freezing mixture. The advantages were twofold: the contents of the moulds could not be contaminated, and the front door could be opened from time to time to inspect whether the contents of the mould had frozen. The patent mentions that the Ice Cave had an alternative use of keeping food hot. Instead of the ice and salt mixture, the voids in the cave could be filled with boiling water, and the outer insulation would keep the contents hot instead of cold. Marshall's ice caves came in four standard sizes: advertisements for the Ice Cave tell us that the smallest held a one-quart mould and the largest six large champagne bottles – yet another use for this ingenious device.

By 1885, the dynamic Agnes Marshall was running her cookery school and her employment agency as well as designing freezing machines and ice caves. In addition, she found time to write her first book, *The Book of Ices*,[40] which was self-published by Marshall's School of Cookery in the summer of 1885. An advertisement in the *Illustrated London News* of 25 July tells us that the book is "now ready" and is available "post-free 2s. 6d., or of any Bookseller".[41] The author of the book is stated simply to be "A. B. Marshall" and not Mrs. A. B. Marshall which is the title she used for her subsequent books. It is a lovely little book, illustrated with colour plates of the finished ices shaped by pretty moulds. Some of the moulds are especially elaborate and take on the form of a pineapple, a swan, a fish, a basket of fruit, a hen and a host of other shapes. The colour plates were produced by the lithographer Raphael Thomson whose premises were at 69 Wells Street, just around the corner from the cookery school.

The book was aimed at a readership from the established middle classes. Making ice cream added to the cook's duties, so it was probably made only in households with more than one servant in the kitchen. In addition, the mistress of the house would need to be wealthy enough to own a freezing machine and the fancy moulds required to make the recipes.

The Book of Ices is short; the early editions run to a mere forty-four pages plus an index and advertisements. There is no preface or introduction – the book launches straight into "Hints on making ices" which comprises seven bullet points:

1. Too much sugar will prevent the ice from freezing properly.

2. Too little sugar will cause the ice to freeze hard and rocky.

3. If the ices are to be moulded, freeze them in the freezer to the consistency of a thick batter before putting them in the moulds.

4. If they are to be served unmoulded, freeze them drier and firmer.

5. Broken ice alone is not sufficient to freeze or mould the ices; rough ice and salt must be used.

6. Fruit ices will require to be coloured according to the fruit. For Harmless Colours see p. 63. [advertisement for Marshall's food colouring]

7. When dishing up ices, whether in a pile or moulded, it will be found advantageous to dish them on a napkin, as that will not conduct the heat to the bottom of them so quickly as the dish would.

There is a postscript to the hints for making ices in the form of a plug for the cookery school which reads:

> Those who wish to be proficient can save themselves a great amount of time, trouble, and anxiety, as well as expense of materials, by attending at Marshall's School of Cookery on any day arranged for "Ices," when they will see the whole system in different branches practically taught, and be able to work from any recipes with ease.[42]

Before the recipes begin, Agnes gives instructions on how to freeze the cream mixture in a Marshall's Patent Freezer, moulding and keeping ices, using a saccharometer, and buying moulds for ices. The kitchen equipment is featured in advertisements at the end of the book with a recommendation that each piece should be bought from the cookery school.

The instructions for making the ices are clear and straightforward as can be seen from the following recipe for making Custard for Cream Ices – Very Rich:

> 1 pint of cream, a quarter of a pound of castor sugar, and 8 yolks of eggs.
>
> Put the cream in a pan over the fire, and let it come to the boil, and then pour it on to the sugar and yolks in a basin and mix well. Return it to the pan and keep it stirred over the fire till it

thickens and clings well to the spoon, but do not let it boil; then pass it through a tammy, or hair sieve, or strainer. Let it cool; add vanilla or other flavour, and freeze. Mould if desired. When partly frozen, half a pint of whipped cream slightly sweetened may be added to each pint of custard.[43]

The book gives recipes for a variety of cream ices made with custard, cream, jam, fruit and syrups, and for making sorbets, mousses, iced soufflés and what Agnes calls "dressed ices", which include bombes, iced puddings and a selection of savoury ices including the curious-sounding Soufflés of Curry à la Ripon.

Agnes Marshall's *The Book of Ices* became the classic book on making ice cream in the Victorian era and sold more than 21,000 copies over the following thirty years. Weir points out that that "prior to 1900 there were very few books written exclusively on ices or ice cream" – the only other British book being Thomas Masters' *The Ice Book*, published in 1844.[44] The success of the book established Agnes as a pioneer in Victorian ice cream making.

During 1885, Marshall's School of Cookery extended its range of activities to become involved in outside catering. The school now had a dedicated catering department which was able to provide the entire service for dinners, banquets, balls and wedding breakfasts.[45] The cookery school was thriving. According to Alfred, there were around 10,000 pupils being taught at the school in the year to October 1886 – a phenomenal rate in growth from a business that was only three years old and which had attracted no students whatsoever in its first few weeks of opening.[46]

Table Talk

Agnes and Alfred were not content merely to expand the teaching and catering side of the business; they had greater ambitions. On Saturday 12 June 1886 they launched their own newspaper with the title of *The Table*, which sold for three pence. *The Table* described itself as "A Weekly Paper – Cookery, Food, Gastronomy, Amusements, &c.,". The newspaper ran to sixteen pages plus a grey cover that featured advertisements. It stated that it was edited by "A. B. Marshall, Marshall's School of Cookery" – so Agnes had now added the title of editor to her other roles as cookery teacher, caterer, inventor and author. Curiously, the paper constantly refers to the editor as "him", and when addressing contributors to *The Table* regarding their manuscripts, it mentions the amount of time the editor has at "his" disposal.[47] Editorials in the paper often refer to Agnes in the third person, for example: "The Recipes of any of the dishes, which are taught in Mortimer Street, and are the outcome of considerable ingenuity and labour on the part of Mrs Marshall and the result of many year's [sic] experience and training, can always be obtained at the uniform charge of 2s. 6d. each."[48]

Whether Agnes was the editor in practice and took on a masculine persona for the sake of convention, or whether she was only nominally the editor is uncertain. My own view is that Agnes and Alfred shared the editorship of *The Table*. The paper began each edition with a feature called "Table Talk" which mixed editorial announcements, news of culinary events, opinion pieces on the latest food topics, and reviews of society functions. Some items were clearly written by Agnes; for example, she writes "I have been asked if I intend to take part in the proposed exhibition at the Aquarium".[49] Other items in "Table Talk" sound as if they were written by a man-about-town, such as a piece in which the writer

(Alfred?) recounts a dinner attended by the Dean of Westminster and records the banter that passed between them concerning William Gladstone, the Prime Minister.[50]

There is no doubt about Agnes Marshall's culinary contributions to the paper. She wrote a weekly column under the heading "New High Class Recipes by Mrs. A. B. Marshall" and another titled "Seasonable and Useful Recipes" which is credited to "A.B.M.". She also penned a column called "The Boudoir Table" in which she writes a letter to an imaginary friend about matters of dining, and which she signs off "Your affectionate AGNES".

A review of *The Table* in the *Aberdeen People's Journal* concluded that the paper was aimed at a higher class of reader, but is generally complimentary:

> We have received the first two numbers of a new weekly paper entitled "The Table" edited by Mrs. A. B. Marshall, the well-known conductor of Marshall's School of Cookery, specially designed for housewives and all others interested in the culinary art. The paper seems to us rather high-class for the ordinary working man's household, as most of the dishes enumerated would require a pretty long purse; but useful tables are given of the retail and wholesale prices current in the London markets for the ordinary articles of household consumption. Pleasant gossipy paragraphs and a short story give a variety to the contents.[51]

The first issue set out the paper's manifesto: gastronomy, cookery and food. The three topics were tackled in some depth but are neatly summarised as "If Gastronomy is simply the science of living, Cookery may lay claim to a place amongst the fine arts."[52]

There is a revealing piece of information published weekly in the section of *The Table* marked "Terms of Subscriptions" from the very first issue onwards. Readers could make annual, half-yearly or quarterly subscriptions to the paper and are advised that "Cheques and P.O.O's. should be made payable to A. B. Marshall".[53] Since cheques were to be made payable to Agnes herself, it implies that she, not Alfred, was the owner of *The Table* and, most importantly, that she held a bank account in her own right.[54]

Considering the above, we can only guess what Agnes must have thought about a piece in *The Globe* newspaper attributing ownership of *The Table* to Alfred.[55] Their columnist writes "Mr Marshall, of the School of Cookery, whose wife was presented early in the season with a 100-guinea locket by her pupils in the culinary art, has brought out a new paper with the happy title of *The Table*." I imagine Agnes was rather more pleased to receive the locket from her students. It must have been a great honour to receive such a valuable gift – a locket bought for one hundred guineas in 1886 would cost about £10,000 to buy today.[56] For a locket as expensive as that, I imagine that several of the pupils' employers also contributed to the fund.

As we have seen, *The Table* contained recipes, menus and dining advice written by Agnes. In addition, the paper listed current retail and wholesale market prices, "table gossip" (in which readers were encouraged to write in with their own tales), short stories, topical discussions on dinners and dining, and amusing anecdotes. The paper featured prominent advertisements for the cookery school, Agnes's books and Marshall's kitchen equipment, but there was extensive advertising from third parties too.

The third issue of *The Table* from 26 June includes a notice that Marshall's had acquired the next-door premises of 32 Mortimer Street in addition to number 30. The school had already upgraded its premises in the spring of the previous year to accommodate the increasing numbers of pupils by adding a "large, new, and specially designed Class-room".[57] A further increase in pupil numbers now prompted the acquisition of the premises next door. At the same time, the school acquired warehouses in Union Place, to the rear of 30 and 32 Mortimer Street, for the purpose of expanding its stores department. The notice assures its readers that "the necessary alterations will not in any way interfere with the business".[58] The need to expand the stores department is significant. Marshall's was already selling groceries from the school, such as gelatine, fruit syrups and flavourings, under its own brand name but it was about to expand its range of goods considerably. Advertisements in *The Table* show us that, in July 1886, Marshall's introduced a new line of culinary moulds which were becoming fashionable at that time. One advertisement shows savoury moulds for sale in the form of a chicken, a ham, a fish and other shapes, and another displays fancy moulds for ices. More importantly, the Patent Freezer and the Ice Cave must now have been in commercial production because the school was selling them to the public along with a new appliance: the "Cabinet Refrigerator".

Although the work involved in launching *The Table* must have been considerable, the cookery school was not being neglected. Agnes was teaching a full programme of lessons, five days a week, that changed weekly, but she also gave an occasional special lecture on what she called an "Entire Dinner Lesson". A notice in *The Table* announced that the last lecture of the season would be held on Friday 2 July before the school closed later that month for its three-week summer break. The programme[59] for a typical week reads as follows:

Monday – popular hot entrées.

Tuesday – ices for dinner and dessert; cream, water and fresh fruit ices; soufflés, &c. – new and pretty designs.

Wednesday – soups, clear and purées.

Thursday – best hot entrées.

Friday – hot and cold savouries.

Pupils at the school could enrol by the day or for a course of lessons. If a student took a course, she was not required to attend the school on consecutive days, but could choose which days she took her lessons as long as the course was completed within two years. Classes started at 10 a.m. and finished around 4 p.m., but the school could provide accommodation if the pupil came from outside London. The school also took on apprentices on three-, six- and twelve-month tenures. It was already claiming to be "The largest and most successful School of its kind in the World" and that "The attendances reach several thousands yearly".[60] The cost of lessons was ten shillings and sixpence for one day's teaching, five pounds and five shillings for a course of twelve lessons, and nine pounds and nine shillings for a set of twenty-four lessons.[61] Five pounds and five shillings was approximately ten weeks' wages for a young cook, so the lessons were not cheap if she was paying for them herself;[62] if her employer was paying, that would be a different matter.

In the edition of *The Table* from 31 July 1886, Agnes announced that she was going to add another section of recipes in addition to the regular "New High Class Recipes". The extra recipes would fall under the title of "Typical English Dinners" (although the series started on 7 August with an alternative title: "Plain English Dinners"). Agnes hoped that the recipes would "add much to the usefulness of our journal in a great number of English homes". Those homes would have been ones that employed what was known as a "plain cook" whose skills (or her employer's tastes) did not extend to making high-class dishes. The new feature started with recipes for Green Pea Soup, Roast Loin of Mutton Stuffed, Brown Caper Sauce, Compote of Pigeons, Carrots in Pea Shapes and Lemon Jelly. It appears that Agnes's recipes, whether for high-class or plain dishes, were extremely popular. There was such a demand for them that people began to write to *The Table* asking for instructions explaining how to make specific dishes. An editorial note in *The Table*'s August editions pleads with readers not to keep requesting new recipes and explains that Mrs Marshall's time was already stretched to the limit preparing for her classes and creating recipes for publication in the paper.

A correspondent from *The Queen* magazine, writing under the name of "La Vieille", visited the school in November 1886 and was greeted by Alfred in his private office. Alfred was concerned that his visitor would not see any *récherché* dishes being made,[63] or an elaborate menu being created because neither were on that day's curriculum. However, the journalist was quite content to watch the breakfast and lunch dishes being prepared and cooked. She described the classroom and Agnes's method of teaching:

> The class room is long and relatively narrow, with a table running the whole length in the centre; on one side a large and very perfectly appointed range, gas stove, and such like appliances; on the other a row of raised seats for such pupils as might choose to sit watching the proceedings and taking notes of the teaching. I may mention that, though everything connected with the cooking was perfect, it was simply such perfection as should be found in all first-class kitchens, whilst every now and then Mrs. Marshall stopped to give little hints as to how the lack of some of the more costly appliances might be achieved. The practical nature of the teaching was what struck me most; unlike so many teachers of cookery, Mrs. Marshall *knows* (and has not simply learnt) her work, and consequently knows how to avail herself of every chance, and gives her pupils the benefit of her knowledge.[64]

"La Vieille" went on to describe the preparation of some of that day's dishes:

> Carefully removing all the skin and sinews and scraping off the white meat, [from a whole chicken] Mrs. Marshall cut the bones into neat joints, and set them aside, to reappear later on

as a delicious grill, floating in a rich tomato sauce. She then took the scraps of flesh, lightly chopped and seasoned them, pounded them with some butter and a little cream, finally mixing in the well-frothed whites of a couple of eggs. They were next rolled into balls, egged and bread crumbed, dropped into the frying basket, and fried a golden brown. Meantime, some white sauce, to which a little cream and some grated Gruyère cheese were added, was thoroughly heated, the chicken balls neatly dished, the sauce poured over them, and carefully browned with a salamander,[65] making an appetising addition to any breakfast table […][66]

The article points out that the school's pupils were from a diverse variety of social backgrounds. There were "ladies taking notes", "simple" cooks and "ambitious young kitchenmaids" who wanted to learn the skills needed to become a "professed cook" (in Victorian times, the term "lady" referred to a woman from the upper end of the social scale – see: Class and Social Mobility). The article was reprinted in full in *The Table*.[67]

The Table was enjoying considerable success. From 30 October 1886, Agnes and Alfred increased the size of the publication by four pages to accommodate more articles and advertisements. In addition, they decided to produce a special edition, *The Table Annual*, in time for Christmas. The annual contained special features on Christmas recipes, menus and stories, prize puzzles, household information and a food calender [*sic*]. The annual could be obtained from "all booksellers, stationers, and railway bookstalls throughout the country" for the price of six pence. Even the demand for copies of back issues was high. Marshall's response was to publish a compendium of all editions of the journal for 1886 at the end of the year which contained all 280 of Agnes's recipes published so far.[68] The success of the journal necessitated a move to its own premises. On 4 December, *The Table*'s editorial, advertising and publishing offices moved from the cookery school in Mortimer Street to a more central location at 2 Newcastle Street, Strand. Once settled in its new offices, Agnes and Alfred decided to give *The Table* a makeover and changed its description to "A Weekly Journal for the Household – Cookery, Food, Society, Amusements".

Advertisements for Marshall's School of Cookery were placed regularly in the daily London newspapers, especially *The Morning Post*. However, in February 1887, a rival cookery school appeared: the International School of Cookery. Not only that, but its premises were on the opposite side of Mortimer Street at number 69. Marshall's response was to amend their advertisements to read "CAUTION. The ONLY ADDRESS – note the number, 30 and 32 Mortimer Street".[69] In reply, the International School of Cookery added "Please note number; the only International School" to their advertisements and reminded readers that the school was "under French chef, late from Boodle's Club".[70] The rivalry between the two cookery schools continued over the coming months. By August, the International School of Cookery was shouting that it was "The ONLY school taught by CHEFS. Mrs. Mackintosh-Smith begs to impress this fact upon the public, that they may not be misled by other advertisements".[71] Marshall's retaliated with "The PUBLIC are CAUTIONED against Persons in the neighbourhood attempting to Trade on the great reputation gained by Mrs. Marshall".[72] The advertising war continued in a similar vein for the rest of the year although it appears that the International Cookery School stopped advertising in early 1888.

Marshall's School of Cookery had other competitors. The National Training School of Cookery (or simply "The National" as it was affectionately known to its alumni) was established in 1874, nine years before Agnes and Alfred bought the Lavenue School of Cookery. The National had influential supporters: the Prince of Wales – the future King Edward VII – was their patron and the Duke of Westminster was their president. Although Marshall's and

The National overlapped in teaching what was called "high class cookery", The National also had a mission to educate the poorer classes in basic or "plain" cookery. The National had its headquarters in South Kensington, London, but, as indicated by its name, it opened satellite cookery schools all over England. In contrast, Marshall's was firmly based in central London. Despite the limited area in which the two schools directly competed with one another, Agnes was a firm critic of The National and, in particular, the way in which it was funded. Agnes wrote a scathing editorial in *The Table* in which she accuses "the authorities in South Kensington" of charging excessively high prices for the catering for the Exhibition of Cookery held that year. The catering was provided by The National from their premises near to the exhibition hall. She continues "If this were a real commercial venture in which the investors might win or lose, nothing would be said; but this is a 'public affair' – so public indeed that its letters pay no postage".[73] Agnes is referring to the fact that The National was partly funded by public money whereas her cookery school was entirely commercial. Agnes believed, with some justification, that The National had an unfair financial advantage.

A petty advertising war and rivalry with other cookery schools did not deflect Agnes from the role of promoting her business. To make her name more widely known, she began to give cookery demonstrations around the country. Agnes put out a call for help and wrote in *The Table*: "During the Summer Vacation Mrs. Marshall proposes to give Practical Illustrations of High Class Cookery in some of the provincial towns, and will be glad to hear from any ladies in any centre, who desire to give assistance in their locality".[74] Mrs Marshall's Provincial Tour (as she called it) travelled to the cities of Birmingham, Manchester, Leeds, Newcastle upon Tyne and Edinburgh during August 1887. The theme of the practical lectures was to be A Pretty Luncheon. A full-page supplement in *The Table* set out the proceedings for the event at the Masonic Hall in Birmingham.[75] Reserved seats were five shillings; unreserved, two shillings and sixpence. General admittance was only one shilling. For their entrance fee, visitors would be treated to a two-hour demonstration of how to prepare and serve a "pretty luncheon" comprising eight dishes. The menu (in French and English) was as follows:

Mayonnaise de Homard à la Gelée	Lobster Mayonnaise with Aspic
Chaudfroid de Pigeons en Caisses	Chaudfroid of Pigeons in cases
Poulet Grille à la Tartare	Grilled Chicken, Tartare Sauce
Soufflé au Parmesan	Parmesan Soufflé
Omelette à la Française	French Omelet [sic]
Gelée au Marasquin	Maraschino Jelly
Petits Nougats à la Chantilly	Little Nougats and Cream
Petites Crèmes de Fraises et Vanille Glacées	Little Strawberry and Vanilla Cream Ices

Each person who attended the lecture would be given the full recipes for all the dishes being demonstrated. The lecture was not only about Agnes promoting the cookery school – she was also keen to demonstrate products sold by Marshall's. The flyer points out that the strawberry and vanilla ices would be demonstrated using Marshall's Patent Freezer and Marshall's Ice Cave, and the aspic and jellies would be made using Marshall's Finest Leaf Gelatine.

A review of the Birmingham lecture was quoted in the following edition of *The Table*. The *Birmingham Daily Post* noted that "there was a large attendance, both of ladies and of persons engaged in the culinary art" and that the audience "went away much pleased with what they had seen".[76]

Agnes's occasional lectures for an Entire Dinner Lesson continued throughout 1887. The final demonstration before the summer break was to be held at the cookery school on 6 May, but the lesson was so oversubscribed that a second demonstration had to be scheduled for three weeks later. A correspondent from *The Queen* newspaper, writing under the byline "S.", was on hand on 6 May to record the event and wrote that "over one hundred cooks and ladies" filled the classroom to capacity. S. explained the format of the lesson:

> The advantage of these "whole dinner" classes over the ordinary lessons is, that one obtains a broad general idea of how a recherché dinner should be served, and also how the various dishes are dovetailed into one another in the making, which is no unimportant matter for "cook". On these occasions Mrs Marshall cooks literally everything required for the day's dinner before the eyes of her pupils of the day, who thus learn practically the sequence of the various dishes, both in the making and the serving.

S. went on to describe Agnes in action:

> It was perfectly wonderful to see how Mrs Marshall kept her head, as she rapidly turned from one thing to another, now explaining and preparing an *entrée*, anon trussing and stuffing up the saddle of lamb, then looking after a sweet, and next getting together the materials for her sorbet, without

flurry or trouble; turning from her own work to help an energetic but not sufficiently enlightened aide-de-camp, explaining away the difficulty, with full particulars, and then returning to her work of demonstration as coolly as if she had simply turned a leaf in a cookery book, instead of carrying every detail and iota of the various recipes in her head.[77]

The lesson was such a success that an engraving depicting the proceedings still featured in advertisements for the school in Agnes's cookery book some eighteen years later. However, there is a cautionary note in *The Table* underneath the timetable of events for the week of the first lecture which reads:

> This will be the last entire dinner lesson given THIS SEASON, in consequence of the great strain which these lessons make on Mrs. Marshall's health. Alterations are under consideration which will more than double the accommodation and relieve the work when the "Entire dinner" lessons will be renewed.[78]

As we know, and despite the announcement, the lesson on 6 May was not the last Entire Dinner Lesson of the season because Agnes repeated the lecture three weeks later. It comes as no surprise that Agnes was exhausted by the proceedings; a press review from *The World* which accompanies the engraving reveals that the lesson lasted for seven straight hours. As regards future arrangements, the engraving clearly shows how crowded the classroom was and the confined space in which Agnes and her assistants had to work, so it is understandable that the format would need to be improved.

The Table underwent some changes with effect from 11 June 1887. The description under the masthead now read "A weekly paper – social & gastronomical". In addition, the format of the paper increased in size and became two and a half inches taller and a little wider. The price of the paper remained the same at three pence, and it was still published weekly every Saturday. Most importantly, Agnes must have withdrawn as joint editor. The issue of *The Table* from 4 June still describes the editor as being A. B. Marshall, as it had done since the paper was launched. However, from 11 June onwards, the editor is no longer credited by name. It is possible that Agnes had already withdrawn from editorial duties when the paper's offices moved to Newcastle Street in December 1886 and that Alfred took over as sole editor at that time.

Agnes's regular column, credited to "Mrs. A. B. Marshall", continued to be published but with the revised title of "New, High-Class, Seasonable and Useful Recipes". The success of *The Table* brought with it some undesirable consequences. It appears that there were some issues with other publications using Agnes's recipes without permission because, in a prominent position between the title and the first recipe, a warning starts to appear stating that "All Recipes are Copyright".

On 8 July 1887, Agnes prepared a banquet for 200 people at Westminster Town Hall. The guests were members of the International and Colonial Congress on Inebriety. A letter from the President of the Congress was published in *The Table* in which he congratulates Alfred for the "elegant, tasteful and truly artistic banquet". Alfred does not receive all the praise; the letter goes on to say that the guests were delighted with "the excellence and variety of the Menu with Mrs. Marshall's new and enticing dishes".[79]

Announcements appeared in *The Table* that Agnes would be giving her lecture of A Pretty Luncheon at Willis's Rooms on two Saturdays in October 1887. As we have seen from the opening paragraph of this book, the first event on 15 October was hailed by the press as a triumph and culminated with the audience of around 600 people spontaneously bursting into applause. The "exclusive arena" of the grand ballroom at Willis's Rooms was transformed into "a temporary kitchen with pots and pans, gas-stoves, and crockery, and crowded by an audience of cooks and enquiring housewives!"[80] Agnes gave the demonstration, which lasted several hours, from a raised platform at the head of the ballroom. Seated tickets were sold in advance from the cookery school. Allocated seats in front of the stage were priced at five shillings; unallocated seats a little further back cost two shillings and sixpence. Tickets costing one shilling were available on the door.

Reviews of the event were published in *The Table*. The best reviews were reprinted over the years in the back of every edition of *Mrs. A. B. Marshall's Cookery Book,* so Agnes must have been especially proud of her achievement at Willis's Rooms. The review from *The Morning Post* reads:

> Watching Mrs. Marshall, it seemed the simplest thing in the world to bone game and poultry, to make purées, sauces, chaudfroids, omelettes, jellies, and ices; but what was done, with consummate ease, at Willis's Rooms must, in the nature of things, have been the result of great patience and practice, combined with the gift of natural dexterity. At the close of the lecture the various plats compounded were exhibited on the platform, and attracted much admiration.[81]

A recurring theme of the reviews for A Pretty Luncheon was how Agnes prepared the meal smoothly and without mess, and how calm and graceful she appeared during the demonstration. The correspondent of the *Leeds Mercury,* reporting on an earlier event, remarked:

> Mrs. Marshall wastes nothing. She does not even waste words. Still less does she waste time. When her luncheon is finished her work is done. There is no litter to clear up. She believes in sending out a meal from the kitchen as neatly as she serves it in the dining-room, and in leaving the kitchen as orderly at the end of her operations as at the beginning. She works, in

fact, without fuss and without stain. The aprons she and her assistants wore yesterday may do for any number of "pretty luncheons". They must have been worn for form's sake. Their protective value was wholly fanciful.[82]

The only review with somewhat negative content came from a surprising source: *The Queen* newspaper, usually an enthusiastic supporter of Agnes Marshall's work. Their correspondent, signing herself E.A.B., was concerned that Agnes "seemed to forget how little many of her audience knew". In other words, that Agnes was assuming that most of her audience had some previous experience in high-class cooking. E.A.B.'s explanation was that the majority of the audience were simple cooks rather than their employers, but perhaps E.A.B was disappointed not to find more ladies like herself in the audience. Despite her misgivings, E.A.B was otherwise impressed by Agnes's demonstration and acknowledges that "every cook and scullery maid will have learned something from Saturday's lecture".[83]

Following her triumph at Willis's Rooms in London, Agnes continued her nationwide tour of A Pretty Luncheon. She started in Brighton on 29 October, and went on to Bath, Cheltenham, Bristol, Reading, Windsor, Exeter, Torquay, Plymouth and, finally, Truro on 21 December.

With the year drawing to a close, *The Table* published an annual edition containing "a food calendar for the year" and "menus of dinners and ball suppers" as well as a host of recipes for "Christmas dainties". The cost of the annual was one shilling. Agnes's last public dinner of the year took place on 31 December at Poplar Town Hall. The dinner was served not to her usual clientele of the middle classes but to the "hungry poor". The guests had been chosen by the local clergyman, the Reverend Bovill, and his wife, and they had originally invited 300 people. However, it is clear from the report that about 400 were eventually fed and yet there were still more hanging around outside the town hall, waiting in vain to be let in. Agnes organised the evening and supervised the cooking of the dinner, while Alfred, the local clergy, magistrates and well-meaning ladies and gentlemen acted as table servers or carved the joints of meat. One dignitary notably absent was the local member of parliament, Sydney Buxton, who made his apologies by telegram. The hall was made available free of charge and local businesses supplied the food, plates and cutlery. Special mention is made in the report of Mr Biggs of the East India Dock Road who cooked the numerous joints of beef and who refused payment for his services. The article comments, rather patronisingly, that "the company were exceedingly well-behaved" even though the guests had been chosen from "the ranks of those really in dire distress". *The Table*'s reporter managed to interview some of the guests and was saddened to hear that one young boy had never tasted beef before and another did not know how to use a fork when eating a meal. At the end of the evening, oranges and sweets were given out to the children and Alfred distributed small packets of tobacco to the men. There is no mention of what the women were given, if anything, but Agnes did promise to send a weekly supply of soup to the area over the winter months.[84]

Brilliant Lectures and a Cookery Book

Agnes's reputation was spreading in illustrious circles. In the January 1888 edition of a prestigious magazine, *The Woman's World*, the editor remarked that "Mrs. Marshall's brilliant lectures are, of course, well known." [85] The editor was none other than Oscar Wilde. He added "I am glad to see that several ladies are interesting themselves in cookery classes." To advance her reputation even further, Agnes had been writing a new book.

Subscribers to *The Table* were advised that *Mrs. A. B. Marshall's Cookery Book* would be published in February 1888. *The Table* informed its readers that it would not be publishing any recipes from the book and reassured them that Mrs Marshall would still be writing original recipes for the paper. Advertisements were placed in the newspapers announcing the publication of the book, but something must have delayed publication because it was not available for purchase until late April. Customers who had pre-ordered the book were advised that their copy would be sent out in the order in which payment had been received. Only when the advanced orders had been fulfilled would the book be available for the public to buy, either direct from the cookery school or from booksellers.

The book ran to 468 pages plus advertisements, and sold for five shillings.[86] It was published by Simpkin, Marshall, Hamilton, Kent & Co. Limited for Marshall's School of Cookery.[87] In the preface, Agnes dedicates the book to her former pupils and assures her readers that "every recipe in it has been successfully carried out by myself, and that I have written each accordingly, and have not copied any from other authors" (see: Was Mrs Marshall the new Mrs Beeton?). The title page of the book gives a stern warning to anyone who might try to copy Agnes's recipes in their own publication that "Infringements of copyright will be prosecuted". The book contains twenty-three chapters,[88] as follows:

> Stocks and sauces
>
> Garnishes, purées, farces [stuffings], &c.
>
> Pastes, icings, glacées, &c.
>
> Hors d'œuvres
>
> Soups
>
> Fish
>
> Hot entrées
>
> Cold entrées
>
> Removes of meat and poultry for luncheon or dinner
>
> Roasts of game for second course
>
> Dishes in place of or to follow game
>
> Dressed vegetables
>
> Breakfast, luncheon, &c. dishes
>
> Sweets, puddings, cakes and breads
>
> Jellies and creams
>
> Savouries
>
> Freezing of ices and iced dishes
>
> Specimen menus
>
> The art of dinner giving
>
> Glossary of terms

English and French names of articles of food

Food calendar

Marketing

The first three chapters of *Mrs. A. B. Marshall's Cookery Book* deal with the building blocks of Victorian high-class cookery – how to make stocks, sauces, garnishes, purées, stuffings, flavoured butter, "pastes" (pastry and batter), icing and glazes. Agnes considered stock, above all, to be the "foundation of all cookery, and on its quality depends almost entirely the excellence of any cuisine".[89] Her stocks fall into two main categories – white and brown. White stocks were made with offcuts and bones of white meat or fish, and brown stocks with red meat or game. Both types of stock would contain a variety of vegetables, herbs and spices to enhance their flavour.

The following chapters contain all the recipes a lady would need to host an elegant dinner party. The chapter headings follow the principal courses for a formal dinner based on the convention of *service à la Russe* which was the fashion in later Victorian times. Agnes gives a basic example[90] for the order of dinner together with a sample menu:

Soups	Consommé Desclignac
	Bisque of Oysters
Fish	Whitebait, Natural and Devilled
	Fillets of Salmon à la Belle-Ile
Entrées	Escalopes of Sweetbread à la Marne

	Cutlets of Pigeons à la Duc de Cambridge
Relevés (Removes)	Saddle of Mutton Poularde à la Crème
Roast	Quails with Watercress
Entremets	Peas à la Française
(Sweets)	Baba with Fruits Vanilla Mousse
(Savouries)	Croûtes à la Française

The above menu (the items in parentheses have been added for clarity) could be supplemented for grander occasions by the other courses mentioned in the chapter headings. *Hors d'œuvres* might precede the soup, dressed vegetables (see below) would accompany the removes, and iced sorbets could be served between the remove and the roast to cleanse the palate.

The terminology used in formal Victorian menus can be quite obscure. Much of the confusion, then and now, comes about because the names of the courses were largely inherited from the earlier convention for fine dining: *service à la Française*. In *service à la Française* there was no sequence of courses that modern diners would recognise as part of, say, a five-course meal. Ian Kelly, in his book *Cooking for Kings*, explains that in *service à la Française*:

> The roasts and highly dressed "grosses pièces" would adorn the table as the guests arrived, along with the side-dishes (entremets) including the centre-piece dessert.

> Twice, the table would be completely reset with plates and cutlery. After the soup there would be a re-lay or relevés of hot fish, and after the roasts and entrées a new re-lay of cold desserts.[91]

As can be seen from Kelly's description, once the soup dishes had been cleared away, there were two further table settings where multiple dishes were placed on the dining table at the same time. The diners would help themselves, and each other, to whatever they fancied. The *grosses pièces* or large joints of meat, would have been ceremoniously carved by the host himself. It did not matter how important the host was. At a dinner cooked by the famous French chef Antonin Carême in 1829 for James and Betty de Rothschild, the richest couple in France at that time, Rothschild himself would have carved the *grosse pièce*.

In *service à la Russe* the various courses were brought to the table one at a time in the same way that you would be served in a modern restaurant. When each course was finished, the plates would be cleared away and the next course brought out hot from the kitchen to be placed before the diners. Agnes's dinner menu above is set out according to this convention.

In Agnes's menu, what she calls the "removes" are the same as the old *relevés,* although what would previously have been a hot fish dish had been replaced by what was the original centrepiece: a large joint of boiled or roasted meat. The *entrées* now follow the soup and the fish (at least in English dining; some French gourmands like Brillat-Savarin preferred to serve their *entrées* after the *relevés*). *Entrées* are what Agnes calls "made dishes", by which she means smaller cuts of meat which had been prepared in some way; for example, coated in a glaze or accompanied by a sauce. The "roast" is translated from the French *rôt*, but confusingly does not signify the traditional English roasted joint of beef or mutton; it is usually a course of game. *Entremets* are small side dishes that can be savoury or sweet depending on their place in the menu. "Sweets" are easily recognisable as sweet dishes, puddings or ice creams. However, there might be an extra course on the menu described as "dessert", especially on menus for ball suppers and wedding breakfasts. In Victorian times, dessert referred to edible table decorations that were intended to impress the guests on their arrival in the dining room, and so were present on the table throughout the meal. Agnes explains that the dessert is comprised of fresh and crystallised fruit, sweetmeats, biscuits and olives artistically presented on the host's finest plates and glassware.[92] The table decoration would have been enhanced by attractive displays of ornamental foliage, flowers and potted plants.

Although Agnes placed emphasis on formal meals with elaborate menus, many of the recipes in the book could easily be incorporated into everyday family meals. In her chapter on The Art of Dinner Giving, Agnes makes it clear that ordinary meals can be created from a shortened version of the menu. She writes:

> This course [the removes or relevés] constitutes the most substantial part of the dinner; it is the grosse-pièce, or the pièce de résistance in the French menu; it is the fundamental centre of the English bill of fare; in fact, in ordinary cases, it forms the dinner with soup or fish as a prelude, and some sweet as a finish.[93]

To add to the usefulness of the book for making everyday meals, Agnes includes a chapter on breakfast and luncheon (lunch) dishes. To the modern cook, many of the recipes in this chapter sound like what we might cook ourselves. Recipes for Devilled Chicken in Pieces (similar to southern fried chicken), Châteaubriand Steak and Fried Potatoes (steak and chips/French fries) and Fried Sole Breadcrumbed (breaded fish) sound familiar enough, although the ingredients for Fried Ox Ears in a Piquant

Sauce might be a little difficult to source from your local supermarket.

The chapter titled "Dressed Vegetables" might need a little explanation. Dressed vegetables are not plainly cooked vegetables such as boiled carrots, but are vegetable dishes that are served with a sauce or that have been cooked with other ingredients; for example, Potatoes à la Princesse (a type of potato croquette), and French Beans à la Crème (green beans cooked in a cream sauce).

The book concludes with the following chapters which provide useful hints and information:

Freezing of Ices and Iced Dishes

Specimen Menus

The Art of Dinner Giving

Glossary of Terms

English and French Names of Articles of Food

Food Calendar

Marketing [purchasing ingredients from suppliers]

Although Agnes was at pains to point out that the recipes in the book and those in *The Table* were unique to each publication, some other parts of the book had already appeared in *The Table*. In particular, the chapter on The Art of Dinner Giving is a lightly edited version of a weekly series of the same name published in the paper between 19 February and 21 May 1887.

With her cookery book published, Agnes threw herself back into her cooking demonstrations. She embarked upon a new tour of A Pretty Luncheon in several provincial towns. Her destinations for May 1888 were Leamington Spa, Bedford and Tunbridge Wells. After her short lecture tour in England, Agnes and Alfred travelled further afield. Underneath the programme of events in *The Table*, there is a brief notice announcing that "During the summer vacation Mrs. Marshall will lecture in some of the leading towns of the United States". We do not know how successful the tour turned out to be, but Agnes and Alfred returned from America in late September 1888. *The Table* announced that Agnes would recommence her lectures at the cookery school on 1 October and that she would introduce "various American novelties into her first week's programme".[94] Agnes resumed her countrywide tour of A Pretty Luncheon in November. The venues were the Bijou Opera House in Liverpool and the Temperance Hall in Leicester.

On New Year's Day 1889, Agnes and Alfred conducted their second annual East End dinner for the poor. The format was much the same as the first dinner although the location moved from Poplar to Stepney. They catered for about 400 diners again, but mostly older people who had been chosen by the local clergy. The guests were served roast beef, potatoes and bread, followed by plum pudding (Christmas pudding). It was estimated that each person was served three-quarters of a pound of beef, which is a huge amount and well beyond the normal means of the residents of Stepney at that time. The dinner was followed by entertainments of singing, comedy routines and conjuring. Agnes presented each of the attendees with a parting gift: tea for the women and tobacco for the men.[95]

Advertisements in *The Table* show that the cookery school had expanded its range of goods for sale. Their specialities were fruit and liqueur syrups, concentrated essences, "superfine" jelly bags, leaf gelatine and "harmless" vegetable colouring. Mrs. A. B. Marshall's curry powder features prominently in the full-page advertisement and was claimed to be "a curry of exquisite flavor [*sic*], of the kind prevalent in the Madras Presidency".[96] At the top of the advertisement was a list of Marshall's selection of wines and spirits: dinner wine, cooking wine, champagne, whisky, brandy, gin and rum. It seems that Alfred's description of himself as a wine merchant was just as true at this point as it had been before. Marshall's continued to introduce new kinds of catering equipment. An advertisement from June 1889 announced that "Marshall's Slicer" was now available to buy. The machine had a large revolving cutting disc containing four adjustable blades, and was operated by turning a handle and feeding in whatever foodstuff needed to be sliced. The machine would slice a variety of vegetables as well as sausages and dried meats. The price was seven shillings and sixpence, and for that money the buyer would acquire "the most rapid, economical, and perfect slicer".[97]

Agnes's charity work took a different turn in April 1889. Instead of cooking for the poor, she had been invited to give a "practical lecture on high-class cookery" to an audience of upper-class ladies. The patron of the event was Her Royal Highness The Princess Christian (daughter of Queen Victoria). The lecture, titled "A Tempting Repast", was held at Westminster Town Hall and seated tickets were on sale at ten shillings and sixpence each (about £54 at present-day prices[98]), although cheaper seats were available towards the back of the hall and in the gallery. The proceeds of the afternoon were to be donated to The Board School Children's Free Dinner Fund which provided free meals to destitute children. A report of the event in *The Table* tells us that Agnes's lecture was a great success even though Princess Christian and many of the ladies attached to the royal court were not able to attend because they were in mourning for the recently deceased Duchess of Cambridge. Nevertheless, the lecture was well attended by about 300 people who were encouraged to buy the finished dishes to boost the charity's funds. The food that Agnes had made during the lecture was set out in an attractive display and everything was sold. Many hopeful purchasers were disappointed.[99]

A couple of weeks after the success of her charity demonstration, Agnes was involved in a carriage accident and suffered cuts and bruises. Although she was not seriously injured, her classes, which were due to resume after the Easter vacation, had to be delayed by a week so that she could recover sufficiently to continue her work.[100] Agnes may have been cheered up while convalescing by the news that *Mrs. A. B. Marshall's Cookery Book* had sold an impressive 10,000 copies in its first year of publication.[101]

The Table was going from strength to strength. The paper proudly confirmed that it would be available at the Paris Exhibition that year and could be found in the Press Pavilion and at the English Dairy stand. There was more good news: to celebrate the success of *The Table,* there would be a special edition published on 19 October as a "double number" with an additional 10,000 copies printed. A postscript to the notice advises advertisers that they should take note of the expected additional sales and submit their advertisements in good time.

Company Business

In 1890, several changes were made to *The Table*. In February, there was a dispute with its printers, The Hansard Publishing Union Limited, following an editorial in the paper that criticised some of Hansard's business dealings. The printers took exception to the comments and insisted that *The Table* should refrain from further adverse editorials. Agnes and Alfred objected to being censored in this way and sacked the printers before the next edition was due. New printers, Spottiswoode & Co., were engaged immediately and began printing the paper on 1 March.[102]

On 9 May 1890, *The Table* was incorporated as a limited company: The Table Newspaper Company Limited. Seven individuals agreed to buy one £10 share each to establish the company. As would be expected, Alfred was one of the founder shareholders but curiously, Agnes was not. Another shareholder of note was John Osborn Wells, who is described as a "newspaper owner". If the name Wells sounds familiar, it is because John Wells was Agnes's half-brother. If we look at the Memorandum of Association of the company, one of the objects for which the company was established was to "To acquire and take over from John Osborn Wells as a going concern the newspaper called The Table and all other the business [sic] property assets and rights in connection therewith".[103] The Memorandum of Association does not indicate what compensation John Wells received for the transfer of the business, but it is hard to believe that he was anything other than its nominal owner. Ultimately, the rights and assets of *The Table* would surely have been owned by Alfred and Agnes.

Changes to the shareholding of the company on 27 August confirm that Agnes and Alfred were indeed the principal owners of the company and now had an equal shareholding. Further shares were issued and paid for, bringing the total number to 218. The shareholders, now eight in number with the addition of Agnes, were as follows:

Name	Occupation	Shareholding
Alfred William Marshall	merchant	100
Agnes Bertha Marshall	cookery instructress	100
John Osborn Wells	clerk	5
George Girling Capon	wine merchant	5
Claude C. Staniforth	fishmonger	1
Napoleon Ruffin	manufacturer of preserved provisions	3
W. W. Box	solicitor	1
F. D. George	refreshments caterer	3
TOTAL		218

It is interesting to note that all the shareholders, apart from Box, were involved in the catering and hospitality industry. Although John Wells was now described as a "clerk" rather than a "newspaper owner", he authorised the shareholder statement in his capacity as "Secretary" (company secretary). Other documents describe Alfred as "Director" (managing director) of the company and the registered office as being 2 Newcastle Street, which was the address of the publishing and editorial office for the paper.[104] From 10 May 1890, subscribers to *The Table* were advised to make their cheques payable to J. Osborn Wells rather than A. B. Marshall as previously.[105] It is not clear why cheques were to be made payable to an individual – Wells – rather than the new limited company. Announcements appeared in *The Table* to clarify that the paper was now the "sole property" of The Table Newspaper Company Limited.

Not only was Napoleon Ruffin now a shareholder in *The Table*, but he also began to support the paper with advertisements for his "high class delicacies". The advertisements proudly claim that the company was "purveyor to H. R. H. The Duke of Edinburgh" and that its products had won a prize medal in the London Cookery Exhibition of 1885.[106]

With the advent of new printers and a new corporate structure, Agnes and Alfred decided to alter the format of *The Table*. The most significant change was to reduce the price of the paper from three pence to one penny. An editorial suggests that the reduction in price was not so much their own choice, but a move to increase circulation encouraged by their advertisers and requests from potential subscribers for a cheaper paper. The editor adds that "in this levelling age" they believed it was their duty to provide quality "social and gastronomical" content to "the million in place of the favoured few".[107] As part of the changes, the paper lost its grey cover made from thicker paper. The move appears to have been successful. By July, *The Table* had almost doubled its previous circulation.[108] In August, *The Table* changed its description yet again. Instead of "A weekly paper – social & gastronomical" it became "A society journal of fashion, food, finance, and fiction".

The cookery school closed as usual for its Christmas vacation and reopened on 19 January 1891. A notice in *The Table* announced that the school would change its hours from the new term onwards. Instead of classes beginning at 10 a.m., they would now start at 10.30 a.m. "to suit the convenience of pupils coming from the country". In the same notice Agnes made it abundantly clear that she was not the author of a book on savouries, attributed to a Mrs Marshall, after receiving numerous enquiries from readers. She adds (rather sniffily) that the subject of savouries was "fully" dealt with in *Mrs. A. B. Marshall's Cookery Book*. Agnes also announced that a second cookery book – "*Mrs. A. B. Marshall's Cookery Book Vol. II*" – was "in preparation".[109]

Significant changes were made to *The Table* in October 1891. A dramatic announcement appeared in the paper at the beginning of the month that, with effect from 10 October, the paper would be reduced in size to just eight pages, and that "Table Talk", "Acts and Actors", "Fashions Fancies" and various other features would be axed. In a parallel development, John Wells, in his role as company secretary, wrote to the Registrar of Public Companies on 5 October notifying them that The Table Newspaper Company Limited had changed the address of its registered offices from Newcastle Street to the cookery school's premises at 30 and 32 Mortimer Street.[110] We can only speculate as to what prompted these changes. Were the society gossip and fashion pages (the ones that were cut) turning off readers who were primarily interested in articles on cooking and dining? That certainly makes sense given that the notice added that the paper "will in future confine its columns, as nearly as possible, to subjects appertaining to 'Cookery', 'Food', 'Household', and kindred matters".[111] Confirmation of *The Table*'s readers' approval of the new format was given in a notice from 7

November stating that "The Manager is pleased to acknowledge the numerous letters approving of the change made in this paper by omitting Society Gossip, &c.".[112] It is interesting that the notice was issued by the manager (John Osborn Wells) and not the editor (who, presumably, was Alfred up to this point).

The paper's new format no longer had a description of its contents on the front page, but it did still include Agnes's page of recipes. That page is the only one to acknowledge Agnes by name. Other articles are uncredited or written by named individuals, in particular Elsie Garth and Mrs E. Allen Simpson. It is noticeable that the paper was now being written predominantly by female correspondents. The new format and style of the paper seems to have brought success. In December that year, there had been problems for some readers in getting hold of their copies of the paper. A notice appeared on 26 December apologising for the lack of availability and promising to forward copies when any returns had been received from wholesale agents. The notice claimed that the shortfall was due to unusually high demand and that the regular number of copies had been printed. Demand had apparently been increasing steadily since "the omission of all extraneous subjects" in October.[113]

At some point between 21 August 1890 and 8 November 1895 (the two dates when the company filed its official shareholding statement in accordance with the prevailing Companies Acts), there was a fundamental change in the shareholding of The Table Newspaper Company Limited. A further seventy shares were issued in the company. The recipient of those shares was "Agnes Bertha Marshall, cookery instructress". What that means is that Agnes had become the majority shareholder because she now owned one hundred and seventy shares while Alfred still owned one hundred shares.[114]

We can only guess at what prompted this momentous change in the balance of ownership. Agnes was a director of the company, along with Alfred, so she already had a day-to-day input in the running of the business. Her books were selling well, her cookery demonstrations were increasingly popular, and the cookery school was thriving. It is possible that Agnes had grown in confidence and was keen to assert herself, having realised that she was the greatest asset in the whole enterprise. If so, Agnes's newly found assertiveness may have provoked some sort of power struggle with Alfred, with Agnes insisting on a greater say in how the business was conducted. That scenario sounds even more likely if the issue of Agnes's additional shares coincided with the major changes to the newspaper's content and the relocation of its registered office back to the cookery school's premises in early October 1891.

A national census was taken on Sunday 5 April 1891. We have already seen that Ethel and Agnes Alfreda Marshall were living at a boarding school in Brighton. According to the census, Agnes and Alfred were living over the shop at 30 and 32 Mortimer Street along with their sons Alfred and William (now ten and eight years old respectively). On the night of the census, they had five female servants living with them and two visitors described as cooks, who were probably students boarding at the cookery school's premises. The servants were a scullery maid, a kitchen maid, a parlourmaid and two housemaids, all of whom were born in Ireland. One other person lived there: Ada Wells, whose occupation is described as "housekeeper". So, not only was Agnes employing her half-brother John as manager of *The Table,* but also her half-sister Ada in her own household.

According to John Deith, Agnes started negotiations to buy property in Pinner, Middlesex, in 1890. He writes: "*The Towers* was an estate of some seven and a half acres". He stresses the point that Agnes bought the estate "with her own money".[115] The Middlesex Deeds Register confirms that a property in Pinner was acquired by Agnes Bertha Marshall on 31 March 1892.[116] Agnes is described on the deeds as "the wife of Alfred William Marshall of Mortimer

Street […] merchant" rather than the successful author, cookery teacher and business owner that she had become.

Agnes became the owner of "all that messuage or dwelling house together with the gardens lawns orchards plantations yards and outbuildings and the several closes or pieces of meadow land containing together by admeasurement by the recent Ordnance Survey thirty one acres […] and being at West End within the hamlet of Pinner".[117] An additional parcel of land, known as Garden Meadow, was also part of the conveyance, making Agnes the owner of an estate of thirty-six acres in total. The house is not called "The Towers" on the deeds, so Agnes must have coined the name after she had extended and improved the original farmhouse.

The Married Women's Property Act had become law in 1882, so Agnes would have been entitled to own property in her own right. However, it was a highly unusual state of affairs in Victorian England for a woman to be the sole owner of the marital home. Later newspaper reports of Alfred's involvement with local organisations suggest that The Towers was Alfred's property, so the fact that the house and estate were owned by Agnes was not general knowledge in the local community. We can only guess why ownership of The Towers was arranged in this way. It is possible that if Agnes's increased shareholding in *The Table* was the result of some sort of power struggle with Alfred, then purchasing The Towers in her sole name would have been a more extreme example of a change in the balance of their relationship. An alternative suggestion, made by Terry Jenkins in his essay in *Petits Propos Culinaires*, is that Alfred might have "wished to avoid any close attention to his own financial affairs which, in the light of his previous conviction and imprisonment for fraud, could have been an embarrassment".[118]

Agnes and Alfred did not move into The Towers straight away. The reason for the delay is clear from contemporary newspaper reports: the old farmhouse was being completely refurbished and the gardens landscaped. There were notices in the local newspapers requesting bricklayers to apply to the Foreman of Works for employment at The Towers. A local newspaper printed a report from a coroner's enquiry into the death of one of the workmen who had fallen from scaffolding in July 1894. The nature of the work was stated to be "alterations and additions to the house". A witness stated that they could not take the injured man into the house because "The owner was not home at the time, and there were only female servants in the house. All the rooms were in disorder."[119] It appears that Agnes and Alfred had moved into the house by this time, even though the renovation work had not yet been completed.

Mrs. A. B. Marshall's Cookery Book continued to sell well. By the end of 1891, 20,000 copies of the book had been published.[120] As usual, Agnes had been busy. An advertisement in *The Morning Post* of 16 November announced that *Mrs. A. B. Marshall's Larger Cookery Book of Extra Recipes* was "in the press" and would be published "shortly".[121] As with her first cookery book, there was a short delay in the actual publication of the book. It was not until January 1892 that the book was available to buy in bookshops or direct from Marshall's.[122] The price was one guinea[123] or twenty-two shillings by post. The book lives up to its name: it is a heavyweight which runs to 656 pages plus forty pages of advertisements. It contains 284 illustrations.[124] The title page proudly announces that the book is dedicated "by permission" to H.R.H. Princess Christian. In her preface (and subsequent advertisements), Agnes was keen to point out that the book did not contain any recipes that had appeared in her first cookery book which she identifies as "Volume I.". She adds "anyone using this work will require to refer to Volume I. for standard sauces and other things given therein". Agnes assured her readers that she had made every dish contained in the book herself and could "vouch for the accuracy of quantities, time of cooking, and other details".[125] All the engravings in the book were guaranteed to have been drawn from dishes that she had made in her classroom.

Mrs. A. B. Marshall's Larger Cookery Book of Extra Recipes is divided into chapters based on categories of dishes. The chapters are as follows:

> Sauces
>
> Hors d'œuvres and savouries
>
> Soups
>
> Dressed fish and fish entrées
>
> Hot entrées
>
> Cold entrées
>
> Breakfast and luncheon dishes and curries
>
> Removes and roasts
>
> Dressed vegetables and meagre dishes
>
> Salads and sandwiches
>
> Hot sweets and puddings
>
> Cold fancy sweets
>
> Fancy jellies, creams, and cold puddings
>
> Dishes with pastries, pastes, rice, etc.
>
> Buns, breads, cakes, biscuits, and dessert sweets
>
> Jams, preserves, compotes, and macedoines of fruits
>
> Pickles and preserves of vegetables and meats
>
> Garnishes, farces, purées, icings, etc.

It is clear from the chapter headings that the book is purely a collection of recipes. Agnes was not offering any advice on menu planning, buying ingredients or preparing basic items such as stocks, as she did in her previous cookery book.

The illustrations in the book are mainly small drawings of the finished dishes. Many of the dishes seem excessive by modern standards and are elaborately presented. For example, Larks à la Czarina depicts a dish of eleven larks assembled in a circle.[126] The birds, heads still attached – with eyes removed – are stuffed, coated in breadcrumbs, fried, and moulded into shape to make them look like pears. My favourite illustration in the book is larger than most and covers almost a whole page. It depicts a female cook wearing a full-length dress and starched apron, standing on a chair, spinning strands of sugar – which almost reach down to the floor – with what looks like a magic wand.[127]

Reviews of the book were positive. The reviewer for *The Dundee Courier* thought that the book was "a more ambitious work" than Agnes's previous cookery book and that it was "doubtless intended for the 'upper ten' of society".[128] Even so, the reviewer reassured readers that:

> No cook, however, need have the least tremor of soul or terror that her efforts with one or any of them [the recipes] will not turn out according to her heart's desire, or come to an unsuccessful end, for Mrs. Marshall has proved every recipe given in the book, and can therefore vouch for the accuracy of quantities, time of cooking, and other details.[129]

The review in *The Queen* newspaper was fulsome in its praise for the book:

> It is certainly, both for the variety of its contents and the perfection with which it is got up, the finest specimen of English cookery literature that has hitherto appeared. The

> illustrations are a study in themselves, and are fully equal to those in the best French cookery books [...]
>
> It may be safely asserted that any cook who possesses both this lady's books need never be at a loss for variety, or in trouble as to the method of preparing the dishes given, for if the directions are only faithfully carried out, success is a certainty.[130]

With her new book published, Agnes resumed her cookery teaching. She continued to demonstrate her Entire Dinner Lesson and gave the last one of the season on 5 August 1892 before the cookery school closed for its summer break. A journalist from *The Queen* attended the lesson and reported in some detail on the food that was cooked, remarking that "Mrs. A. B. Marshall certainly possesses the art of making the most both of her time and her materials with regard to flavour and appearance".[131] The reporter mentioned that the cookery school had recently been refurbished. Some new classrooms had been added and others had been enlarged, although it is not clear how the extra space had been made available. A new ventilation system and electric lights had been installed, and parquet flooring had been laid throughout the premises, even in the large rooms in the basement used for packing goods. The report ended with the news that Agnes would be giving lectures during the summer in Liverpool, Manchester, Leeds, Newcastle upon Tyne and Edinburgh.

Marshall's School of Cookery regularly took out full-page advertisements in *The Queen* and other journals, giving details of the services it offered. The list is extensive and provides a useful summary of Agnes and Alfred's business affairs in the early 1890s. The advertisements display three pictures: the cookery school from the outside, the showroom for kitchen utensils and the showroom for culinary moulds. The stores department announces that it would send, on request and post-free, catalogues for culinary dainties and special goods, culinary and kitchen requisites, moulds, and wines, spirits and liqueurs. A résumé of *Mrs. A. B. Marshall's Larger Cookery Book of Extra Recipes* is prominently displayed, and a smaller space gives information on *The Book of Ices* and *Mrs. A. B. Marshall's Cookery Book*. Details are given for the times and arrangements of classes and there is an invitation to request a prospectus. There are several notices for services provided by Marshall's: cookery lessons from "lady teachers" given in private residences; "professed cooks" for catering at banquets and functions; a comprehensive array of kitchen and table equipment for formal events; and the engagement of permanent and temporary cooks through the school's employment agency.[132]

By January 1893, *The Table* had started to expand once again, and had increased its page count to twelve pages from eight. Its price was still one penny and subscribers' cheques were still payable to J. Osborn Wells. The paper's content remained primarily related to cookery and dining, as it had done since the extensive changes made in October 1891.[133]

Agnes was busying herself with a new lecture tour which she titled "A Tempting Repast". She gave the lecture in Sheffield, Hull and Scarborough in early January 1893. Once she returned from her tour, Agnes resumed her lessons at the cookery school. If visiting the London classroom was not convenient, the school announced in *The Table* that it could send "certified teachers" to any organisation, or even to private families, around the country to give a course of "high-class cooking lessons".

Exhibitions

I imagine that Agnes Marshall was the sort of person who enjoyed a challenge, and her next culinary adventure was certainly ambitious. She decided to demonstrate the preparation, cooking and serving of a complete ball supper for one hundred people. The "Ball Supper Lesson" was a considerable step up from her regular Entire Dinner Lesson. Marshall's advertisements prior to the event describe it as "the most important cookery lesson ever given", which is quite a claim to live up to. The preparation and cooking took place over two days (28–29 March 1893) in the new classroom at the cookery school. *The Queen* reported that a capacity audience of 170 students were present for the demonstrations.[134] Each pupil, who had paid a course fee of ten shillings and sixpence, was given a full menu and printed recipes for all thirty-six dishes made over the two days.[135] Agnes's original intention was to display the finished meal in the same classroom on the evening of the second lesson. Pupils would be allowed to view the display for free, but the public would be invited to buy tickets at two shillings each. The response to the sale of tickets was overwhelming; Agnes had to hastily relocate the venue for the evening's display to the largest hall in the Cavendish Rooms, which were opposite the school's premises in Mortimer Street. A newspaper report of the evening's proceedings indicates that the room was so crowded that the attendees were instructed to walk slowly around the huge table which held the display and were tactfully encouraged to move along if they stayed in one spot for more than a few minutes. "Thousands of ladies" were reported to have visited the display.[136]

The evening was promoted as an unmissable social event and Agnes's influence was such that she succeeded in attracting some eminent partners. Mappin and Webb provided the plates; F. & C. Osler, the glassware and china; and Messrs. Chilton, the floral decorations. All three firms were top establishments in London (F. & C. Osler were glassmakers to Queen Victoria[137]) where a lady might buy the essentials for a high-class dinner party. The table was decorated exactly as if it was on display at a ball supper. The thirty-six dishes made in the school's classroom were tastefully laid out and the table was decorated with hundreds of flowers arranged in Osler's cut-glass bowls. Agnes greeted her guests at the start of the evening and gave special thanks to her three partner firms. A correspondent from *The Queen* described the table setting and enthused that "everything was most beautiful and artistic, from the delicate and quaintly shaped glass and china to the beautiful plate".[138] As to the food, the reporter noted that "Mrs. A. B. Marshall [...] appears to have been generously anxious to set before her public as many as she could of the dainty dishes suitable for such a festivity". It was common practice at the time to include impressive set pieces as part of the ball supper; the table at the Cavendish Rooms was enhanced by some, but they were bought in rather than made as part of the lesson. The reporter wrote: "as *pièces de resistance* there was a boar's head and a pyramid of pressed and spiced beef prepared by M. Ruffin". It sounds like Agnes was calling in some favours that evening because M. Ruffin is none other than M. Napoleon Ruffin who, as we have seen, was a shareholder in *The Table* and one of its advertisers.

The edition of *The Table* published on 22 April contained a supplement dedicated to the Ball Supper Lesson. On the evening of the display at the Cavendish Rooms, but before the public were allowed in, Agnes arranged for a professional photograph of the full length of the display table to be taken by Bedford Lemere, which was a leading English photography studio of the era. The image of the ball supper table was reproduced as a full-page supplement accompanying the paper. The picture shows the table, which was 40 feet (12 metres) long, laid out with floral arrangements, candelabra and place settings. There are potted palms decorating the room, and the whole scene looks very grand. The paper quotes several glowing reviews of the event taken from prominent newspapers from London and around the country. The review from *Truth* reads "There was such an immense crowd at Mrs. A. B. Marshall's display, that it was with considerable difficulty that we could see the table. It was worth some trouble, however, for it was quite lovely". *The Leeds Mercury* wrote "In all respects it was perhaps the most remarkable table-display ever seen in London" – high praise indeed.[139]

The Table underwent yet another format change on 24 February 1894. A new cover was introduced, and the number of pages was increased by four to sixteen; the price remained at one penny. A new and lengthy description of the paper appeared under the title. It reads: "Cookery and Gastronomy. The House and Home. Table Decorations. Dinner and Diners. Culinary Echoes. Foods and Drinks. The Markets. In Paris. Menus. &c." The comprehensive new coverage still included the page featuring Agnes's recipes. Judging by the new style and content, it appears that the paper had a new editor although no name is given. A new contributor appears in early 1895 in the form of someone calling themselves Diner Out (also Diner-Out). Their "Across the Table" column started on 26 January and continued for over ten years. The column is reminiscent of the old "Table Talk" which was axed in October 1891. Quite why the editor chose to reinstate what was considered at the time to be an unpopular feature is unknown, but I can hazard a guess.

I suspect (having looked through every weekly edition of *The Table* from over sixteen years) that Agnes Marshall took over as editor of *The Table* for a second time in October 1891: the period in which fundamental changes were made to the content of the paper and the shareholding of the company. Agnes probably relinquished the role in February 1894 and Alfred returned as editor. Alfred then commissioned Diner Out's "Across the Table" column to replace the original "Table Talk" feature which Agnes had dropped during her second stint as editor. It may be that this was Agnes and Alfred's way of restoring some balance in their business relationship.

Diner Out's identity is examined in more detail in the chapter: Memorials and Myths. My conclusion is that it was definitely not Agnes, and it may even have been Alfred himself. Whoever Diner Out was, they had a passionate dislike of the vegetarian movement that was growing in popularity at the time. There are regular articles over several years ridiculing vegetarians in "Across the Table". One acerbic article reads:

> A bomb has been thrown into the vegetarian camp by Sir Henry Thompson, who has hitherto been freely quoted by the bean brigade, as he has always maintained that everybody eats meat too frequently. […] After this the vegetarians may well take a back seat, in fact Sir Henry Thompson even denies their right to the name by which these fanatics describe themselves, since, as he points out, they are really mixed feeders, milk and eggs being animal products.[140]

In another, Diner Out makes sarcastic remarks about London's vegetarian restaurants being closed on Good Friday:

> It is sad to think that there may even now be hundreds of hitherto 'faithful vegetarians' dining in quite a respectable manner 'from the joint,' all on account of their inability to obtain their accustomed diet of grass and beans for one day during the holidays. And yet the vegetarians would have us believe that man is not a carnivorous animal![141]

During the period in which Agnes returned as editor, there were no such attacks on vegetarianism. On the contrary, there is a thoughtful article written by E. Allen Simpson published in

November 1891 titled "Vegetarianism" which reports on the forty-fourth anniversary of The Vegetarian Society. The article sets out the menu for the anniversary dinner and states "it may doubtless be interesting to many of our readers to study the vegetarian dinner which was enthusiastically enjoyed by the 130 guests present" (presumably including Mrs Allen Simpson herself). The article goes on to publish the recipes for various dishes served at the dinner and concludes that "several of our readers may have pleasure in trying them".[142] The tone of the article provides a striking contrast to the antagonistic attitude towards vegetarians displayed in the column written by Diner Out.

The critical and financial success of the first Ball Supper Lesson prompted Agnes to repeat her triumph in May 1894. The format of the lesson was essentially the same although she did add a new feature to the proceedings: a cooking competition between current and former pupils of the cookery school. Each competitor had to produce an entrée, a savoury and a sweet, and the winning dishes were put on show during the evening of the event alongside the ball supper. The correspondent for *The Queen* newspaper commented that the gold and silver medal winners' efforts were worthy of Mrs Marshall herself, which must have made Agnes proud of her students and her own teaching.[143]

Agnes had been busy writing her fourth (and final) book: *Fancy Ices*. The book was published in June 1894 and according to one reviewer "should be very useful to confectioners and cooks in large establishments".[144] *Fancy Ices* has a striking cobalt blue cover with icicles hanging down from the title font and an embossed picture of a polar bear holding a tray of moulded ices while standing on an iceberg, all presented in a striking silver colour. The book cost ten shillings, and runs to 238 pages plus another thirty pages of advertisements. It displays eighty-six illustrations. Agnes's Introduction confirms that none of the recipes in the book are duplicates of those from *The Book of Ices,* and that *Fancy Ices* is intended for more advanced cooks wanting "more elaborate styles of service".[145] The chapters in the book are as follows:

General ices

Individual ices

Soufflés, mousses, and biscuits

Sundries

The book was not as popular as *The Book of Ices*; by 1909 (see: Publication Dates for Agnes Marshall's Books), only 3,000 copies had been published compared to 16,000 for *The Book of Ices*.[146] Interestingly, the picture from *Mrs. A. B. Marshall's Larger Cookery Book* of a uniformed cook spinning long strands of sugar while standing on a chair is repeated in *Fancy Ices*; the instructions for spinning the sugar are virtually the same.

In June 1894, Marshall's introduced a new product to its range. It was called Luxette and is described in advertisements as a "dainty purée" which had been "prepared by A. B. Marshall". The paste came in an earthenware terrine which, in turn, was sealed in a tin container. As a result, Luxette had a long shelf life, and was available from retailers and by post from the cookery school. Marshall's would, on request, send out a free pamphlet of Agnes's recipes using Luxette as an ingredient. It is hard to tell what the purée tasted like because, unlike today, there was no list of ingredients on the packaging, although later advertisements describe it as a type of fish paste. It was promoted as suitable for "breakfasts, luncheons, picnics, sandwiches, hors d'œuvres, and savouries".[147] The advertising was true to its word – Agnes had used Luxette in sandwiches and a savoury dish, which she called *Crèmes de Luxette à la Marlborough,* in her Ball Supper Lesson the previous month. More dishes based on Luxette featured in Agnes's third Ball Supper Lesson that took place on 10 and 11 April 1895 and followed a similar format to her previous Ball Supper Lessons.

A revised and enlarged edition of *Mrs. A. B. Marshall's Cookery Book* was published in April 1895. The new edition contained the entire contents of the previous one plus over one hundred extra recipes and fifty-five additional illustrations. Publication marked the sale of 30,000 copies of the book and, despite the increase in content, it still sold for its original price of five shillings. A novel promotion for the new edition was advertised in *The Table* and in other newspapers. If the owner of a previous edition of the cookery book, "no matter how old or torn the old copy may be", returned it to the manager at the cookery school, they would be provided with a copy of the new edition completely free of charge, except for the price of the postage.[148] By this time, the *Larger Cookery Book* had sold 4,000 copies and *The Book of Ices*, 8,000 (see: Publication Dates for Agnes Marshall's Books).

An advertisement for Marshall's School of Cookery from March 1896 provides further insight into Agnes and Alfred's business affairs. They had recently bought the commercial rights and trademark for Cowan's Baking Powder. In January, they had engaged a public analyst, Cecil H. Cribb B.Sc. F.I.C., to assay the baking powder, and his summary gives a glowing report of its properties and purity. Marshall's was now manufacturing and packing the baking powder itself, and made a special introductory offer to its customers. Each drum of baking powder contained a coupon marked "large", "medium" or "small", depending on the size of the drum. Customers could collect the coupons and redeem them in exchange for Agnes's books. Fifty large coupons would buy *Mrs. A. B. Marshall's Cookery Book* and twenty-five, *The Book of Ices*. One day's lesson at the cookery school could be purchased in exchange for 105 large coupons. If collecting so many coupons was beyond an individual's reach, the advertisement suggested that "friends can club together and secure the benefits".[149]

Agnes scheduled her fourth annual Ball Supper Lesson for December 1896; it was the most extensive event held yet. Announcements appeared in *The Table* from as early as September giving details of the format. There were to be the usual demonstration lessons on the first two days and then an exhibition and cooking competitions on the following two days. The Ball Supper Lessons were to be held in the main classroom at 30 Mortimer Street on 15 and 16 December. Tickets cost ten shillings and six pence for each day. Ticket holders would be given a copy of the full menu and recipes for all the dishes being demonstrated. Pupils wishing to attend were encouraged to buy their tickets well in advance because the demonstrations were likely to sell out. Thirty-six dishes were prepared during the lesson which were subsequently set out in an attractive display at the exhibition.[150]

The third and fourth days were dedicated to a Cookery Exhibition and Ball Supper Display. As part of the exhibition, there were five cookery competitions. Entries for the first competition were restricted to past and present students of Marshall's School of Cookery. The participants had to cook three dishes – a cold entrée, a sweet dish and a savoury dish – taken either from *Mrs. A. B. Marshall's Cookery Book*, Agnes's recipes published in *The Table,* or dishes that Agnes had demonstrated in her classes. The first prize was three guineas. Agnes also sponsored a second competition which was open to all comers. Contestants had to make a cake and a "loaf of fancy bread" using Cowan's Baking Powder (which was, of course, owned by Marshall's). First prize was one pound.[151]

The other three competitions were sponsored by regular advertisers in *The Table*: Liebig's Extract of Meat Company, J. S. Fry & Sons (chocolate) and The Eagle Range and Foundry Company. The competitors were required to make use of each company's products in their respective competitions. The entrance fee for the first day of the exhibition was two shillings for the afternoon session and one shilling in the evening. The charge for the final day was one shilling all day from 11.30 a.m. to 9.30 p.m. Pupils who had paid to attend either of the two lessons received a free ticket to the exhibition.[152]

It is clear from the partnership with sponsors and the entrance fees that the event was as much a commercial venture as a publicity exercise for the cookery school. Stalls were set up at the exhibition to display goods sold by Marshall's School of Cookery, Messrs. Fitton & Co. (the makers of Hovis bread) and the three main sponsors mentioned above. Advertisements appeared in the London and provincial newspapers promoting the event from October onwards. Cooks who were interested in entering the competitions were invited to write to the cookery school requesting an entry form.

The exhibition was held at Queen's Hall, Langham Place, which had opened three years earlier as London's principal concert hall.[153] As with previous events, table decorations were provided by another partner, in this case Messrs. Piper & Son. To make the day as pleasant as possible for the visitors, Karl Kaps' Palace Band entertained them with a repertoire of light music.

The event was highly successful. *The Queen* newspaper, reporting on the two lessons, pronounced that "it is very certain that in Mrs. A. B. Marshall, London possesses one of the cleverest cooks going".[154] *Truth* magazine reported that 1,500 people attended the exhibition on the first day alone and that Agnes's thirty-six dishes were supplemented by set pieces designed by "Monsieur Marquis, the well-known French chef". One of the chef's creations was a truffled turkey and, not to miss a business opportunity, he was selling his bottled truffles and other specialities from his own stand at the exhibition.[155]

By the mid-1890s, Agnes and Alfred had settled into their new home in Pinner. Alfred, in particular, was beginning to involve himself in local affairs. He was appointed vice-president and captain of the local volunteer fire brigade, and he offered to donate one hundred guineas to start a fund that would be used to build a fire station. The donation was offered "on behalf of Mrs. Marshall and myself" and gratefully accepted by the President of Pinner Fire Brigade.[156] In the spring of 1896, Alfred put himself forward and was subsequently elected as a member of Pinner Parish Council. In his statement following his election, he acknowledged that he had "not been a long resident in the neighbourhood" but assured the parishioners that he would conduct his duties for the benefit of the community.[157] Alfred was not content with being a mere parish councillor for long. In June 1898, he stood for election as a county councillor and was duly elected.

Agnes continued to teach her classes at Mortimer Street, which means that either she was commuting into London every day or was staying over at the cookery school on weekdays. There was a Metropolitan Railway station at Pinner, which opened in 1885, and was within walking distance of The Towers.[158] So it was relatively convenient to travel into London. We know that the Marshalls also used the station at Harrow[159] because a personal advertisement appeared in the *Harrow Observer* on 6 October 1896 reporting that a monogrammed carriage rug had been lost on the journey back from the station, and that the finder would be "well rewarded" if they returned it to the coachman at The Towers.

Being one of the most important property owners in the local area came with additional responsibilities to the community. There are numerous newspaper reports of Agnes and Alfred hosting fetes and garden parties on their estate, but one of the most elaborate took place on Saturday 21 August 1897. Alfred had invited eight of the local fire brigades to a rally at The Towers, which coincided with Alfred's fiftieth birthday and added a further dimension to the celebrations. The various fire brigades marched through Pinner in full uniform led by the Pinner Brass Band. The arrival of the procession at The Towers was the signal for the garden party to begin. Amusements were provided, including a coconut shy, and two marquees had been erected for the refreshments. There was a certain amount of segregation of the guests: one marquee was designated for the dignitaries and Alfred's personal guests, and the other was for the regular firemen. The guests were encouraged to wander around the gardens, and many took full advantage. The *Harrow Observer* remarked upon the sight of "the uniformed firemen in caps of helmets, and their more diversely and gorgeously clad lady friends who had come to share in the afternoon's amusement".[160] Music was provided by Karl Kaps' orchestral band as a background to the evening's festivities.[161] It appears that Agnes did not organise the catering; that was the preserve of Mr Cross of The Cocoa Tree public house who made sure that the firemen and their partners were generously fed.

At the end of the meal, the local clergyman proposed a toast to Alfred and Agnes and revealed that it was Alfred's fiftieth birthday that day. The crowd cheered and sang "He's a Jolly Good Fellow" in response. Later in the evening, the firemen were requested to light lamps which had been distributed around the grounds. The lamps were lit simultaneously when the order was given so the whole garden was illuminated at once. The firemen then conducted a torchlit procession around the grounds while carrying multi-coloured torches. The finale to the evening was an impressive firework display which lit up the summer night sky to the delight of the assembled audience.

It is clear from Alfred's birthday celebrations that he and Agnes were, by this time, wealthy people. They were affluent enough to send their son Alfred William to Rugby School, the prestigious public school.[162] The Towers was a grand house with grounds that boasted extensive lawns, flower gardens and orchards. The census of 1901 reveals that they could afford to support a staff of six live-in servants: a housekeeper, a cook, two housemaids, a scullery maid and a butler. The butler, the housekeeper and one of the housemaids were German; another of the housemaids was Austrian. The presence of a butler confirms Agnes and Alfred's wealth and status. Male servants were more prestigious because they were paid considerably more than females, and because their employer had to pay a tax on their services.[163] In addition, Agnes and Alfred employed outdoor staff to run the estate. There was a coachman for the stables and a head gardener, each of whom would have been responsible for several junior staff. It is worth remembering that all the employees at The Towers would have been paid out of Agnes and Alfred's private funds, unlike the staff at the cookery school who were instrumental in generating profits for the business.

The benefits of having the resources to employ domestic staff sometimes came with unenviable duties. On one occasion, Alfred discovered that their cook had been stealing property from the house and felt duty-bound to report her to the police. The subsequent court case was reported in some detail in the local newspapers. The cook, Bridget Gilhooly, had been employed at The Towers for over four years, and at Mortimer Street before that. When questioned by the police, she confessed to the theft of various articles belonging to the Marshalls including cutlery, silverware and fabrics. At the trial at Edgware Petty Sessions, Agnes was called as a witness to identify the stolen property. Alfred testified as to the cook's previously good character with the result that the magistrates decided to deal with the matter themselves and not refer the case up to the Quarter Sessions. Gilhooly was sentenced to three months' imprisonment "without hard labour".[164]

By 1897, Agnes's involvement in *The Table* seems to have diminished. Her name appears only on the page featuring her "New, High-class, Seasonable, and Useful Recipes". Even here, the recipes do not always fill a whole page as before, and sometimes only stretch to half a page. But if Agnes had taken more of a back seat at *The Table*, she was still firmly in charge of the cookery school. After the Christmas break and the outstanding success of her fourth Ball Supper Lesson and Cookery Exhibition, she reopened her cookery classes on 18 January and demonstrated her first Entire Dinner Lesson of the year on 14 April. The cookery school attracted a steady flow of students through its weekly newspaper advertisements. Agnes's first three books continued to sell well. The *Cookery Book* had, by now, sold 35,000 copies; *The Book of Ices*, 10,000; and the *Larger Cookery Book*, 6,000. It seems that *Fancy Ices* had proved not to be as popular as Agnes might have hoped. In October, she published a new edition of the book (the second thousand) and reduced the price from ten shillings to five shillings.[165]

Marshall's was, as usual, active in promoting itself and took part in the Victorian Era Exhibition of 1897 at Earls Court in October. The company won a gold medal at the exhibition for its "kitchen utensils and culinary requisites".[166] The kitchen equipment displayed at its stand went on sale at the cookery school after the exhibition closed. The moulds, kitchen utensils, freezers, ice caves and refrigerators were sold at reduced prices even though they were guaranteed to be new and unused (although it was noted that they may have acquired minor blemishes during the exhibition). *The Table* published a full list of the items for sale.

Marshall's continued to produce its own products. By the end of the 1890s it had registered five brand names other than its own: Luxette, Cowan's Baking Powder, Coralline Pepper, Sildeen Consommé and Silver Rays White Rum. Having registered names was sometimes not enough. It seems that Agnes's personal name was being used without her permission in connection with other people's demonstrations and for the promotion of gas stoves. Warnings appeared in *The Table* urging caution that "Mrs. A. B. Marshall has no connection whatsoever with any Gas Stove Exhibitions, and does not give any lessons away from her establishment in Mortimer Street".[167] However, Agnes did lend her name to some useful promotions. A regular advertiser in *The Table*, the Liebig Company – manufacturers of beef extract – organised a cookery competition with *Mrs. A. B. Marshall's Cookery Book* as one of the prizes, The judge of the competition was C. Herman Senn who was a respected culinary expert and, unsurprisingly, Agnes was happy to have her name associated with such a prestigious contest. The other prizes included Senn's own book, *Senn's Practical Gastronomy*, and the best-selling *Mrs. Beeton's Book of Household Management*. So Agnes was in good company.

By the beginning of 1900, Agnes's books had clocked up further impressive sales. The *Cookery Book* had sold 45,000 copies; *The Book of Ices*, 12,000; the *Larger Cookery Book*, 7,000; and *Fancy Ices*, 2,000 (see: Publication Dates for Agnes Marshall's Books).

Unfortunately, Agnes met with an accident on 22 December 1900. She was still convalescing "under doctor's orders" in January 1901 and had to delay the resumption of her classes following the school's Christmas vacation.[168] It was not until 17 February that she was fit enough to resume her teaching. That term's lessons ended on 3 April with a special version of Agnes's Entire Dinner Lesson in which she demonstrated some new dishes that she had discovered on a recent trip abroad. The lesson was sold out and was later reviewed favourably in *The Queen*, *The Lady's Pictorial* and *Madame* magazines.

Family Matters

At the time of the national census on 31 March 1901, Agnes and Alfred were living at The Towers in Pinner with their daughter Agnes Alfreda who was twenty-one and single. Agnes gives her occupation as "teacher of cooking" and Alfred describes his as "manufacture culinary requisites". Both are classified as employers. Alfred was fifty-three at the time of the census and Agnes claims to be forty-four, taking one year off her age compared to the previous two censuses (and probably four years from her true age – see: Memorials and Myths).

What of Agnes and Alfred's other children? Ethel, now twenty-two, had married a man named Albert Newman in 1900 and they were living in Holland Park Gardens, Kensington. Alfred Harold was now twenty and William Edward, eighteen. They were both absent from The Towers on the night of the census.

The census shows that John Osborn Wells was now married and living in Redcliffe Road, Kensington. He and his wife, Catherine, had one servant in their household. John's occupation is given as "manager of cookery school and general stores", which confirms that he was "The Manager" of Marshall's School of Cookery frequently referred to in *The Table*. His sister Ada was no longer living with Agnes and Alfred as their housekeeper as she had been ten years previously.

The records of The Table Newspaper Company Limited confirm that Agnes and Alfred were still the sole directors of the company as of 8 August 1901. Alfred is described as "merchant" and Agnes as "cookery instructress". There seems to have been some confusion as to what address they should use for the official Register of Directors. Firstly, they recorded their addresses as The Towers, Pinner. Then, they crossed out those entries and wrote 32 Mortimer Street over the top as the correct address.[169]

The dawn of a new century brought no distinctive innovations for Marshall's School of Cookery or *The Table*. The newspaper advertisements for the cookery school continued in much the same format as before. *The Table*'s content, format and description were still the same in 1905 as they had been since the major changes introduced in February 1894. An updated edition of the *Larger Cookery Book*, which had by now sold 8,000 copies, was published in February 1902. The frontispiece was still graced with the portrait of Agnes that had appeared in the first edition of the *Cookery Book* in 1888. The exact same press reviews of Agnes's lectures from 1887, which had appeared in the first edition of the *Cookery Book*, were still being published in the new editions and in those of the *Larger Cookery Book* among the advertisements (although the year in which the reviews were written had been discreetly removed).

The shareholding of The Table Newspaper Company Limited had remained constant since Agnes had become the majority shareholder. The first change in over ten years reflects a tragedy that was about to unfold. On 30 June 1905, Agnes transferred her entire shareholding to Alfred. It must have been clear to them both that Agnes was mortally ill, and it seems that they organised the transfer of shares while it was still relatively straightforward to do so.[170]

Agnes Bertha Marshall died of cancer on 29 July 1905. Her death certificate records that the cause of death was "Carcinoma. Syncope." Carcinoma is cancer and syncope is fainting fits. She died at home at The Towers with Alfred by her side. Alfred is described on the death certificate as a manufacturer of comestibles. Agnes is merely described as his wife, despite her widely acknowledged fame and accomplishments. The certificate states that she was fifty years old.

Agnes was cremated at Golders Green Crematorium and her ashes were buried in Pinner Cemetery. There was a funeral procession through Pinner village to the sound of muffled bells followed by a burial service at the church. Mourners at the service were noted in a local newspaper as being "Mr. A. W. Marshall (husband), Mrs. Newman and Miss Marshall (daughters), Mr. W. Marshall (son)", along with friends, local dignitaries, and staff from The Towers. There is no mention that Alfred junior attended the service, although that may be an error of omission.[171]

Throughout her teaching career at Marshall's School of Cookery, Agnes had made a point of informing prospective students that it was she alone who gave the lessons at the school. The last ever notice to read "Mrs. A. B. Marshall personally conducts her classes" appears in the Programme of Work published in *The Table* on 6 May 1905. She must have been too ill to work after that. Agnes conducted her last Entire Dinner Lesson on 4 November 1904 and the correspondent from *The Queen* pronounced it a great success. The reporter wrote of Agnes that "in her hands every cookery process looks so easy that it is only after leaving the classroom, and perhaps rashly making culinary experiments oneself, that one fully realises the amount of work got through and knowledge possessed by this *cordon bleu*".[172]

It is likely that Agnes realised the seriousness of her illness as far back as late 1904. A fundamental change took place in the ownership of The Towers – the deeds show that sole ownership of the property was transferred from Agnes to Alfred on 6 December.[173] The deed was signed by Agnes and witnessed by her solicitor, William W. Box (who also happened to be a shareholder in The Table Newspaper Company).

It may be that Agnes's cancer diagnosis prompted her and Alfred to instigate some financial planning in the event of her death to minimise the potential tax burden. A new tax called Estate Duty had been introduced in the Government's Finance Act of 1894 to replace the previous system of death duties. Unfortunately for Alfred's tax affairs, the new Act specified that a gift from one person to another was only free of tax if it had been made at least one year before the death of the donor. Agnes died less than eight months after gifting The Towers to Alfred.[174]

Astonishingly, there is no mention whatsoever in *The Table* of Agnes Marshall's illness or her death. There is no obituary for the person who was the school's founder, driving force and key to its success. Nor was there an obituary for Agnes in *The Queen* newspaper which had championed her and her cookery demonstrations right from the beginning. I suspect the two are connected. Because Agnes **was** Marshall's School of Cookery, and had always been presented as such, the school would have needed to play down the unfortunate truth that its principal was no longer around to run the show. Pupil numbers might have declined, and the circulation of *The Table* decreased if too much attention had been drawn to Agnes's untimely death. Alfred probably had a word with his contacts at *The Queen* and agreed a mutually beneficial arrangement.

However, several obituaries were published in other newspapers. *The Cheltenham Examiner* wrote:

> The untimely death of Mrs. A. B. Marshall, of the School of Cookery, will be a great shock to her many friends and admirers. After some weeks of much suffering she passed away early on Saturday last, and with her the workaday world has lost a gifted woman of rare personality, sympathetic and kind-hearted to a degree.[175]

The *Truth* newspaper wrote:

> She possessed that not very common gift, a discriminating and sensitive palate. Men often say that women have no palate, but, if so, there are a few exceptions to the rule, and Mrs. Marshall was a notable one. Her Friday class, to whom she gave a practical demonstration of cooking a whole dinner of many courses, was a *tour de force*. I saw her once on an

occasion of the kind. She stood in the centre of a long table, which was surrounded by cooks of almost every age and size, and her manner was as quiet, her gentle smile as composed, as though she were merely preparing tea for a few friends.[176]

There is an illuminating comment from *The Cheltenham Examiner*'s correspondent, who clearly knew Agnes well and appears to have been a long-standing friend, about the success of Marshall's business. They wrote:

> It is over twenty years since Mrs. Marshall began her pioneer work in domestic cookery in Mortimer-street and there I first saw her teaching her class of professional cooks and amateurs, a work which grew to large proportions, and was the foundation of the important business her husband, Mr. Marshall, developed, and which is now known wherever the English language is spoken.[177]

The above paragraph confirms that Agnes and Alfred brought their respective talents to the Marshall's enterprise. While Agnes taught her students, gave demonstrations and wrote cookery books, Alfred ran the business side of things and handled the merchandising.

A year after Agnes's death, Alfred and the family attended a service in Pinner Parish Church where a memorial window was dedicated in her honour. The stained-glass window consists of two panels: one depicting St Agnes and the other St Bertha. At the base of the window there is a dedication which reads "In memory of Agnes Bertha Marshall, born August 24th, 1855, died July 29th, 1905".[178]

Two months later, on 27 September 1906, Alfred remarried in Christ Church, Woburn Square, London. His new wife was Gertrude Mary Walsh whom Deith claims had previously been Agnes's personal secretary, but who had been dismissed by Agnes following allegations of an affair with Alfred.[179] At the time of the marriage Alfred was fifty-nine and Gertrude was thirty-three. On 19 August 1907 Gertrude gave birth to a daughter at The Towers; they named the baby Rosalie Osborn. They continued to live at The Towers and Alfred remained active in the local community, helping to establish the West End Lawn Tennis Club in 1910. Previously, the club's tennis finals had been held on the grass courts at The Towers. Alfred continued to be a benefactor of the club – he paid for a pavilion to be built in 1912 and a new hard court in 1914.[180] Although Alfred and Gertrude were still living at The Towers, it seems they had a property in London as well. At the time of the 1911 census, they were living at 21 Sussex Place, Marylebone, together with six servants. Oddly, Alfred is described as a "gelatine merchant" on the census return, even though gelatine was only one of the many products produced and sold by Marshall's. The Towers was demolished in the mid-twentieth century and the land sold to make way for a housing estate.

What did the future hold for Agnes and Alfred's children? As we have seen from the 1901 census, Ethel married Albert Newman in 1900, but the Newmans have proved elusive to find in the 1911 census.

Agnes Alfreda died in August 1935 aged fifty-five. She never married, and left her estate valued at £1,203 to her brother William Edward.[181]

Alfred Harold died prematurely at the age of twenty-seven in 1908. He was living in Bournemouth at the time, and the local newspaper reports that he died of consumption (tuberculosis) after a long illness. He was cremated at Golders Green Crematorium and his ashes were buried next to his mother's in Pinner Cemetery. He had been something of a "wild child" and his court appearances for driving offences were reported on several occasions in local newspapers. In one incident, he had been flagged down by a policeman for speeding across a crossroads but had failed to stop.

Bravely, the policeman jumped onto the running board of the car and forced Alfred to stop! Alfred was fined £1 by the court.[182]

William Edward joined the family business. By July 1915, he had become a director of The Table Newspaper Company Limited; his occupation was described as "manager". He was also a shareholder in the company, owning twenty shares which had been transferred from Alfred's holding. We know this because the total numbers of shares issued still amounts to 288 but Alfred only holds 230. Alfred would have had his original 100 shares plus Agnes's 170, transferred just before her death, giving a total of 270. So he must have transferred twenty to William and a further twenty to a new director: Beatrice Frigout, whose occupation was "secretary".[183]

After Agnes's death, *The Table* carried on much as before. Curiously, the paper continued with her regular column: "Recipes by Mrs. A. B. Marshall". A quick cross-check of the recipes published between Agnes's death and the end of the year produces no matches with the recipes in her two cookery books. So either the feature was using previously unpublished recipes devised by Agnes, or someone else was creating new ones and *The Table* was publishing them under Agnes's name. *The Table* itself continued to be published until 1918, initially under Alfred's management and later under his son William's.[184] The Table Newspaper Company Limited went into voluntary liquidation in November 1921 and was wound up as a company.[185]

Marshall's School of Cookery had a longer lifespan than *The Table* and continued trading until the outbreak of the Second World War in September 1939. Its premises at 30 and 32 Mortimer Street no longer exist; a new building was erected on the site in 1958.[186] It is possible that the original buildings suffered bomb damage during the war – there is a record of high explosive bombs falling in the locality in the period between October 1940 and June 1941.[187]

Agnes's books carried on selling well, long after her death. In the year that she died, *The Book of Ices* had sold 14,000 copies; the *Cookery Book*, 55,000; the *Larger Cookery Book*, 8,000; and *Fancy Ices*, 2,000.[188] Her books continued to be promoted in *The Table* and in the cookery school's newspaper advertisements. Four years later, the books had sold 16,000; 65,000; 9,000; and 3,000 copies respectively. An advertisement in the last edition of *The Book of Ices* published before the copyright was acquired by Ward Lock (see: Was Mrs Marshall the new Mrs Beeton?) shows that 21,000 copies of *The Book of Ices* and 75,000 of the *Cookery Book* had been published. There is no mention of the *Larger Cookery Book* or *Fancy Ices,* so it is possible they had been discontinued by this time. An advertisement in the book confirms that the cookery school was still conducting daily classes under the title of "A. B. Marshall's Lessons", but that *The Table* had shrunk to being published bi-monthly instead of weekly.[189]

We have seen how Agnes Marshall's cookery school flourished and how well her books sold, but what was she like as a person? Contemporary accounts give us some idea. Her obituary in *Truth* reveals that:

> In appearance, she was the last person in the world who would be taken for a cook. She was a pretty woman, of a Spanish type, with large, dark, kindly, and expressive eyes. Her figure was slight and graceful.[190]

The Cheltenham Examiner paints a picture of Agnes's appearance while she was conducting her lectures:

> Often I have gone to see Mrs. Marshall cook an entire dinner, from soup to dessert. On these occasions, as whenever exercising her art, she wore her dainty lace and muslin apron, with deep fine muslin cuffs, and always the handsome diamond locket presented to her by her pupils some years past

as a token of gratitude and love. At the end of the demonstration, every dish cooked by her own hands, there would not be a speck or stain on her toilette, and the table was as orderly as if just out of the manipulation of the 'redder-up'.[191] [192]

The paper's correspondent goes on to describe Agnes's later years:

It was a strenuous life, and the success, great as it was, was made by hard and continuous attention to business, for it was only in later years that she allowed herself the ordinary pleasures of Society. Her chief pleasure, however, was welcoming her friends to her hospitable house near Pinner, a charming retreat, bright with flowers, and homely with many and various pets.[193]

The Bridget Gilhooly court case reveals that Agnes was a generous person who donated her unwanted clothes to her servants. Agnes was asked by the judge about the matter, and she confirmed that she did give away clothes but never table linen, which is what was discovered in Gilhooly's personal boxes. Agnes clearly earned the admiration and devotion of her students, as evidenced by the fact that relatively low-paid cooks could raise enough money to buy an expensive locket.

Although the name of Agnes Marshall is not as well known today as that of, say, Isabella Beeton (see: Was Mrs Marshall the new Mrs Beeton?), she was famous in her own time. An amusing article in *The Field*, a newspaper for country sports enthusiasts, instructs its readers that, to encourage pheasant chicks to eat, first they should throw down some food for the hen pheasant. The writer explains that "this food need not be of the extra 'Francatelli' or 'Mrs. Marshall's School of Cookery' quality".[194] To have Agnes's name linked with the renowned Charles Elmé Francatelli, who was chef to Queen Victoria and a number of prestigious London clubs, in a casual remark reveals just how great a celebrity Agnes had become by 1887.

A fitting summary of Agnes Marshall's accomplishments comes from the correspondent for *The Queen*, reporting on her Ball Supper Lesson from 1894:

> Mrs. A. B. Marshall's name is not to be made by this time; her skill and talent is generally acknowledged; but this exhibition of her pupils' work shows her in a new light, as the foundress of a really superior school of culinary art, and one which should rank her name among the best known *cordons bleus* – an honour alike to her sex and her nation.[195]

Memorials and Myths

Memorials

Agnes Marshall was a pioneer of Victorian ice cream making. Her recipes and teaching enabled the middle classes to emulate their social superiors using her affordable and labour-saving machines. However, in her lifetime she was better known for her teaching and cookery demonstrations than for her expertise in making ice cream, even though that is how she is best remembered today. She did teach lessons on making ice creams and sorbets at her cookery school, but they were, on average, once every three weeks. She gave lessons every weekday, so that means only about one lesson in fifteen was concerned with ices.

It is encouraging to see that Agnes Marshall has become better known in recent times. Her profile was raised in 1976 by the writer and celebrity cook Fanny Craddock. She wrote a book titled *The Sherlock Holmes Cookbook* in which she imagines Sherlock Holmes's cook, Mrs Hudson, to be writing a cookery book in her retirement which features Holmes' favourite dishes. Craddock's Foreword reveals that she was an admirer of Agnes Marshall and that many of the recipes in the book were inspired by Marshall's own recipes. Craddock writes:

> Here was this character, Mrs Hudson, cooking for two men during the heyday of the Victorian era, an era which already contained special appeal for me since it gave us the woman who wrote everything contained in *Escoffier's Guide to Modern Cookery* some years before this masterpiece of his was published.
>
> The name of this lady was Agnes Bertha Marshall. Her story will be told in another book upon which I am still working

> *The Great Marshall Mystery*, and it is a mystery, since this beautiful, socially eminent cook was, to imitate Mrs Hudson's style – A Most Remarkable Woman whose origins (and demise) are wrapped in deepest mystery!
>
> I have borrowed from her writings and associated her in the most tenuous terms with Mrs Hudson.[196]

I hope that this book has resolved at least some of the mystery surrounding Agnes Marshall's origins (and demise). It is a shame that Craddock never published *The Great Marshall Mystery* because it would have given us a fascinating insight into her view of Marshall's work. The fictitious Mrs Hudson thinks of Agnes Marshall as her "Great Ideal". She relates a story of when she visited Marshall's School of Cookery in Mortimer Street "to make a small purchase" and was thrilled to see Marshall herself working at the desk in her office.[197]

One of my culinary heroes, Elizabeth David, mentions Agnes in her book *Harvest of the Cold Months*. She writes:

> Moulds for them [shaped ice cream dishes] were still current up to the time of the 1914 war, and were illustrated in trade catalogues and in the advertisement pages of books such as those of the famous Mrs Agnes Marshall, whose cookery school in Mortimer Street, London, flourished in the 1890s and 1900s.[198]

A major work on Agnes Marshall's life and accomplishments was published in 1998 with the title *Mrs Marshall: The Greatest Victorian Ice Cream Maker*. It is widely regarded as the seminal work on Agnes Marshall, and I have quoted from it here on numerous occasions. The book is the work of several contributors – Robin Weir, John Deith, Peter Brears and Peter Barham – whose essays were originally presented to the Oxford Symposium on Food and Cookery in 1995.

Early Years

Mrs Marshall: The Greatest Victorian Ice Cream Maker has brought Agnes Marshall to life for a new generation of cookery scholars. It is an invaluable book and a rich source of information on Marshall. However, some of the assertions by John Deith regarding Agnes's background and early years have been challenged in recent times by subsequent researchers.

An essay by Terry Jenkins, published in the journal *Petits Propos Culinaires*, suggests a completely different background for Agnes from the one recorded by Deith in the above book.[199] At the time of writing, Jenkins has updated Agnes Marshall's Wikipedia entry to reflect his findings.[200]

As we have seen in the first chapter, Agnes's mother, Susan Smith, declared herself to be a "spinster", not a widow, on her marriage certificate to John Wells. If that statement is accurate, Agnes's declaration on her own marriage certificate – that she was the daughter of John Smith – cannot be true unless John Smith and Susan Smith were unmarried but coincidently shared the same surname. The weight of evidence suggests that Agnes invented John Smith some years later to give the impression that she was the daughter of a lower middle-class clerk to whom her mother was married at the time of her birth.

Jenkins suggests that the reason why other researchers (including myself) have not been able to find Agnes's birth records is that they were looking in the wrong year. He claims that "her birth certificate shows that her name was Agnes Beere Smith, and that she was born on 24 August 1852 at 14 Silurian Terrace, Haggerstone. The day and month were as expected, but she was three years older than she claimed".[201] He proposes that the "Beere" part of the name was in fact the surname of Agnes's true father, and that she changed her middle name to Bertha some years later to disguise her ancestry.

The lack of evidence that Agnes was born in 1855, as she claimed, does not necessarily mean that she was the Agnes Beere Smith who was born in 1852 (I know from researching my own family history that searching for a common name like Smith can produce many hopeful but ultimately false results). There are some anomalies in Jenkins' theory. I have seen a copy of the relevant birth certificate, and the date of birth is recorded as 25 August 1852, **not** 24 August – the day on which Agnes celebrated her birthday. Admittedly, the birth certificate is only one day out, and the birth was registered sometime later on 4 October, so a mistake could have been made. Nevertheless, the birth dates do not match exactly. In addition, as mentioned in the opening chapter, the suggestion that Agnes was born in 1852 does not tally with the age she stated on the 1881 and 1891 census returns, and the age that her family declared her to be on her death certificate and memorial window.

Jenkins has searched the census records and has successfully found Susan Smith, a dressmaker, living with her one-year-old daughter, M S W Smith, in Hackney. As we have seen, Agnes's mother, Susan, did have a daughter by John Wells who was named Mary Sarah Wells Smith and who would have been a year old in 1861. However, Agnes (who would have been eight years old if she was born in 1852), was not living with her mother on the night of the census. The census does record that an Agnes Smith, aged eight, was living with her grandmother, Sarah Smith, in Walthamstow. Agnes stated in later censuses that she was born in Walthamstow which was then in the County of Essex. Haggerstone was located in the Shoreditch District which was in the County of Middlesex. Why would Agnes change the place and even the county of her birth? Jenkins suggests that, because Agnes was brought up by her grandmother in Walthamstow, she adopted the location of her early years as her place of birth.[202] So was Agnes Beere Smith, born in 1852, the girl who became Agnes Bertha Marshall? The evidence thus far is plausible.

Agnes Beer[e] Smith reappears in the official records in 1878 to register the birth of a daughter named Ethel, born on 27 April in Hackney, Middlesex. Agnes Beer Smith is described as an unmarried domestic servant, and the baby's full name is given as Ethel Doyle Smith. Once again, Jenkins ascribes the child's middle name to be the surname of the father. The date of birth does fall within the time period established from Ethel Smith/Marshall's later census records. The coincidence of the family names – an Ethel Smith being born to an Agnes Smith who was the daughter of a Susan Smith – gives greater credence to Jenkins' theories, and I think he may well be right.

For me, the most interesting aspect of Agnes's early life is the circumstances surrounding her first daughter Ethel. As we have seen in the first chapter, it is almost certain that Ethel was born in 1878 while Agnes was still single. If Jenkins is correct, Ethel's father was a man named Doyle, not Alfred Marshall as previously thought. The question is, when did Alfred discover that Ethel existed? Surely not after he and Agnes were married – that would have been a startling revelation. The most likely explanation is that Alfred knew about Ethel all along because Agnes had told him when they first met. On the other hand, if Jenkins' theory is wrong, then Alfred himself is likely to have been her father. In both cases, the existence of a child born to unmarried parents would not fit well with Agnes and Alfred's aspirations of becoming respectable, middle-class businesspeople. So they farmed out Ethel to Agnes's mother and stepfather for the sake of appearances. How they introduced her into their own family sometime later without people asking awkward questions is anyone's guess.

Why would Agnes lie about her age on the censuses and why did Alfred state her age as being fifty (meaning she was born in 1855) on her death certificate and on her memorial window if she was really born in 1852? If Agnes had taken three years off her age when she first met Alfred to appear younger than she really was, he would have had no reason to disbelieve her (their marriage certificate merely states their ages as "full", which means that they were both over twenty-one and did not need parental consent to get married). If that is true, she would have been obliged to continue the deception when filling out the census returns. We know that Agnes took a further year from her age for the purposes of the 1901 census, so she was clearly flexible about such matters.

Myths and Mistakes

As far as I have been able to discover, Agnes Marshall's sobriquet of "Queen of Ices" is a relatively recent acquisition. Mark Kurlansky,[203] Charlotte Montague,[204] and an article on the BBC website[205] all imply that she was known by the title in her own lifetime. However, I have not been able to find any references using that moniker in contemporary Victorian newspapers. None of the authors in *Mrs Marshall: The Greatest Victorian Ice Cream Maker* calls her the "Queen of Ices". Instead, the essay by Robin Weir affectionately describes her as "Ice-Cream-Monger Extraordinary".[206] There is an article in *The Queen* newspaper from 1894 under the heading "Ice Queen", but the report does not give the impression that it was a name by which Agnes was commonly known. It seems to be merely a clever title for a piece about the imminent publication of her book *Fancy Ices*.[207]

The *Encyclopedia of Kitchen History* by Mary Ellen Snodgrass has an entry for Agnes Marshall which, in general, records Agnes's history and achievements correctly. Unfortunately, there are several factual errors in the book which have been repeated by subsequent writers. Snodgrass claims:

> In 1883, she purchased the National Training School of Cookery on Mortimore Street in London, which had been

operated by Felix and Mary Ann Lavenue since 1857. The curriculum, a forerunner of home economics education, offered specialty instruction in cooking, including lessons in curry from an English colonel who had served in India and classes in French *haute cuisine* taught by a Cordon Bleu graduate.[208]

Agnes and Alfred Marshall did buy an established cookery school in 1883 but it was the Lavenue School of Cookery in Mortimer Street, not the National Training School of Cookery in South Kensington. The National was established in 1874 and continued operating until 1962. It was The National, not Marshall's, that was the forerunner of home economics education. Marshall's advertisements were always clear that it was Agnes herself who conducted the cookery lessons at the school, so it is unlikely that her school ever employed a colonel or a cordon bleu chef to give lessons. I can find no evidence in the school's timetable, printed in *The Table*, to corroborate Snodgrass's claim. There are other errors in Agnes's entry in the *Encyclopedia of Kitchen History* including the statement that "She died in Brighton on July 29, 1905, while convalescing from injuries received in a riding accident".[209] The date of Agnes's death is correct, but she died from cancer at home at The Towers, Pinner.

Some cautious speculations by the authors of *Mrs Marshall: The Greatest Victorian Ice Cream Maker* have been repeated by subsequent writers as facts to become modern-day myths. For example, the BBC website tells us that:

> Known as the Queen of Ices, Agnes Marshall opened a school in 1883 where she taught cookery and ice cream making. A true entrepreneur, by 1885 she patented her own mechanical ice cream maker, sold accompanying ingredients and ice cream moulds, and suggested using liquid nitrogen to make

ice cream a century before it became a popular ice cream-making method.[210]

The BBC article is incorrect in saying that Agnes patented the machine because it was patented by her husband Alfred. Deith is careful not to assign ownership of the patents to Marshall's ice cream machine to Agnes, saying only that she "claimed it as her own invention", which it almost certainly was.[211] Agnes's entry in the *Oxford Dictionary of National Biography*, written by Weir, clearly states that it was Alfred who submitted the patents.[212]

The story about Agnes suggesting the use of liquid nitrogen to make ice cream has been widely repeated by others. Its source is undoubtedly the essays by Weir and Peter Barham in *Mrs Marshall: The Greatest Victorian Ice Cream Maker*. The story is partially true, but there are some aspects which make it far less clear-cut than it seems.

Both Weir and Barham[213] quote an article in *The Table* from 24 August 1901 which reads:

> Liquid air will do wonderful things, but as a table adjunct its powers are astonishing, and persons scientifically inclined may perhaps like to amuse and instruct their friends as well as feed them when they invite them to the house. By aid of liquid oxygen, for example, each guest at a dinner party may make his or her ice cream at the table by simply stirring with a spoon the ingredients of ice-cream to which a few drops of liquid air has been added by the servant.[214]

As Barham points out, liquid oxygen and liquid air are completely different chemical substances even though the terms are used interchangeably in the article.[215] There is no mention of liquid nitrogen whatsoever. Even allowing for the author's scientific confusion, liquid oxygen is highly flammable and liquid nitrogen was not available at that time for domestic use. It had only recently been produced for the first time and was used exclusively by scientific establishments. Therefore, the suggestion for the use of liquid nitrogen (or liquid air) in making ice cream is purely hypothetical, even though the author of the article in *The Table* makes it sound as if it was readily available at that time. Barham explains that "a few drops" of liquid nitrogen would be nowhere near enough to freeze a bowl of ice cream. His own experiments have established that "you need to add about a volume of liquid nitrogen equal to about a quarter the volume of ice cream mixture to get it to freeze rapidly and effectively". Barham concludes that "I do not believe she [Agnes] was ever able to obtain the liquid to try out her idea in practice".[216]

Most importantly, was Agnes Marshall even the author of the quote from *The Table*? The article containing the quote is credited to "Diner Out" who, as we have seen, began writing their column "Across the Table" in *The Table* in January 1895. From reading through several years of Diner Out's column and looking at the style in which it is written, I believe that Diner Out was a man (quite probably Alfred Marshall). For example, it is unlikely that a woman would write, regarding the catering at the House of Commons:

> After Whitsuntide it will be neat-handed Phyllises in snowy caps and aprons who will hand strawberries and cream, the tea and cakes, and other dainties with which the sisters and cousins and aunts, and other feminine belongings of the members, regale themselves of an afternoon. [...] Maids in pretty caps and frilly aprons are not only much pleasanter to look at, but they are defter and more alert, and altogether more agreeable about a table than waiters.[217]

Although Agnes might have written the above, however unlikely, she would not have written the following passage credited to Diner Out when discussing mutton chops:

> When you asked for chop at the 'Cheshire Cheese' or Anderton's or any of the old eating-houses, or when you sent to your own butcher's for 'a nice chop', or ordered the same at your club, there came a thick, rich-looking, juicy, well-proportioned and tender portion of sheep. Now a similar demand in restaurant or club or private house brings forth a measly, gristly, ill-flavoured, hard and bony arrangement, and in consequence the chop is losing its hold upon our affections.[218]

I can quite believe that Agnes would be equally dismissive of poor-quality mutton chops. However, no lady (see: Class and Social Mobility) would have dreamed of dining in a chop house such as the Olde Cheshire Cheese in Fleet Street. Chop houses were the preserve of men, and were not considered appropriate venues for respectable women.[219] Similarly, London clubs were strictly male-only environments. Woman were not even admitted into gentlemen's clubs, let alone allowed to use their dining facilities.

It is a fascinating story, but the claim that Agnes Marshall was the first person to suggest using liquid nitrogen to freeze ice cream looks tenuous indeed.

Weir lists what he thinks are Agnes Marshall's greatest achievements in his essay in *Mrs Marshall: The Greatest Victorian Ice Cream Maker*. One of those mentioned is that Agnes was "the first person in the world known to record the putting [of] the ice cream or sorbet in an edible cone or cornet, in 1888".[220] Weir is referring to a recipe from *Mrs. A. B. Marshall's Cookery Book*, which was first published in 1888. The recipe is called Cornets with Cream.[221] Weir's research is confirmed in Kurlansky's book *Milk!* where he debunks the widely accepted belief that invention of the ice cream cone was made by Ernest Hamwi at the 1904 St. Louis World's Fair. He also cites Agnes's recipe from 1888 as evidence.[222] Agnes fills her cornets with vanilla-flavoured whipped cream, but she does suggest alternative fillings which have become the basis of the story. She writes "These cornets can also be filled with any cream or water ice, or set custard or fruits" and "served for a dinner, luncheon, or supper dish".[223] Recent authors appear to have used Weir's essay as a source. For example, in her book *Women of Invention*, Montague writes about Agnes that "She has been credited with inventing in 1888 the first portable, edible ice cream cone called a 'cornet' which was made from ground almonds."[224] However, Agnes Marshall's cornets were not intended to be portable containers for ice cream (which is how we would think of them today) as Montague suggests. Marshall's cornets, with whatever filling, were meant to be eaten at the table, using cutlery, as part of a meal.

In his book, *The Ice Cream Connection,* Ralph Pomeroy goes even further back for the origins of an edible ice cream container. He suggests that the ice merchant and restaurateur Carlo Gatti (see: Ice and Ice Cream) was selling ice creams to take out from his cafés in the 1860s which were served "in 'cornets' made of dough baked in the shape of sea shells".[225] But, as Pomeroy sagely points out, "Histories differ. The history of ice cream seems to differ considerably. Legend and fact meet and part in a kind of dance of persuasion."[226]

Class and Social Mobility

The British class system was (and arguably still is) a minefield to navigate, both as a participant and an observer. In the Victorian era, there were three principal classes: working, middle and upper, but each class had its own sub-divisions depending on the individual's type of employment and their wealth. In her book *Victorian London*, Liza Picard notes that:

> The Victorians liked to have social classes clearly defined. The working class was divided into layers, the lowest being 'working men' or labourers, then the 'intelligent artisan', and above him the 'educated working man'.[227]

The middle class was similarly stratified into lower and upper denominations. The lower middle class were employed in occupations such as clerks, schoolteachers and shopkeepers. The upper middle class included the professions (solicitors, accountants, doctors etc.) as well as business owners involved in commerce and manufacturing. The upper classes encompassed the owners of large estates, senior clergy, the aristocracy and the royal family.

Some social classifications spanned class distinctions. In Victorian society, only those at the higher end of the middle and upper classes would have qualified to be referred to as "ladies" and "gentlemen". Those titles had a specific meaning, unlike today where they merely signify gender, and would not have been applied to a lower middle-class schoolteacher and his wife. Hugh McLeod explains that although lower middle-class men were not gentlemen, they were "gentlemanly". They adopted the appearance and manners of the upper middle classes because they were:

> made up of that part of the wage-earning population which came into direct contact with the established middle class by working beside them in their offices, by handling their money in the banks, by representing them as commercial travellers, or by serving them in 'quality' shops, together with those who moulded the children of the masses in the elementary schools.[228]

McLeod lists what he calls the norms of middle-class life which precluded the majority of the lower middle class from even trying to become ladies and gentlemen. They were "saving, giving their children a good education, contributing to charity, above all, keeping servants, in order to preserve middle class women from the degradation of manual labour."[229]

Sometimes, the Victorians' rigid social structure caused unfortunate misunderstandings. Colonel Arthur Kenney-Herbert, writing as "Wyvern", wrote a book titled *Furlough Reminiscences* about a "happy holiday" in England while on furlough from the Madras Cavalry in India. Kenney-Herbert makes the embarrassing assumption that an attractive and well-dressed French companion in his railway compartment is a lady. He is astonished when it turns out that the object of his admiration is not what she seems. He confesses: "[I] lost my heart for fully two hours to Lady D----'s '*own maid*'!"[230] It is not the French "lady" who gives the game away but her male companion who has been sitting quietly in the corner of the compartment. Although he is equally well dressed, he is in fact Lord D's valet. Because the valet is English, from the moment he starts to speak, his accent tells Wyvern all he needs to know about his social class. Wyvern is shocked that he thought the couple were a lady and gentleman. He writes about the valet: "his roughly-toned, badly-pronounced English completely staggered me".[231]

In her study of social mobility in Victorian Britain, Dr Victoria Powell examines the life of the actor and theatre manager Henry

Irving (1838–1905) who, like Agnes Marshall, came from humble beginnings, and who rose to such a prominent position in society that he was knighted in 1895. Powell explains that:

> […] the Victorians interpreted status through the effect of the presence of the body in social interaction and understood society as consisting of two groups, the polite and the vulgar. As Irving left behind the lower middle-class social circles of his youth that conditioned and constrained his bodily practices, and entered new social circles, he changed the way he spoke, presented himself and moved his body.[232]

Although Powell acknowledges that "in a society in which mobility of a modest nature was all that most people could achieve, Irving's rise was uncommon",[233] there are some parallels with Agnes's own life. Agnes Marshall's association with Princess Christian was a similarly high social accomplishment (for a woman at that time) to Henry Irving being knighted by Queen Victoria. The author Bram Stoker published a biography of Irving in 1906 in which he wrote "He forewent very many of the ordinary pleasures of life, and laboured unceasingly and without swerving from his undertaken course".[234] This sounds very much like Agnes's obituary in *The Cheltenham Examiner* which reads "It was a strenuous life, and the success, great as it was, was made by hard and continuous attention to business".[235]

Victorian men were encouraged to "improve" themselves through self-education. Kathryn Hughes tells us that:

> Author Samuel Smiles coined the term 'self-help' which he used as the title for his best-selling book. *Self-Help* (1859) had chapters such as 'Application and Perseverance' and contained scores of inspirational case histories about men who had risen from humble beginnings to become captains of industry.[236]

However, Hughes warns that:

> This sounds exhilarating, but the price of failure was very high. People who didn't rise in the world were assumed to be at fault. They were seen to be lazy, extravagant, or proud and therefore responsible for their own poverty.[237]

Most women could only improve their social standing by marrying "above" themselves. Alfred's father was a builder, and therefore working class, but because Alfred became an orphan and was subsequently educated by the teachers at the orphanage, he was able to become a teacher himself. That accomplishment would place the young Alfred at the lower end of the middle classes. By transforming himself into a merchant and by raising his status from schoolteacher to private tutor, he climbed into the ranks of the established middle class (conveniently burying his past conviction for embezzlement).

If, as seems likely, Agnes invented John Smith as her father for the purposes of her marriage certificate, she is likely to have done so for two reasons. Firstly, to establish that her mother was married when Agnes was born; and secondly, to give her father, and so herself, the lower middle-class status that went with him being employed as a clerk. Both reasons provide Agnes with a "respectable" background instead of being the working-class daughter of a single mother that she really was. Agnes's mother, Susan Smith, was the daughter of a carpenter according to her marriage certificate when she married John Wells.

Whether Alfred was aware that Agnes's background was not all that it seemed is uncertain. Did he think that she was a lower middle-class girl from Walthamstow? Or did he know that she was the daughter of a working-class single mother from Shoreditch?

Once Agnes had married Alfred, whatever her previous status, she had firmly become a member of the middle classes. She had escaped "vulgar" society. Even so, Agnes's subsequent social success begs a multitude of questions. Did Alfred teach her how to speak and conduct herself properly in "polite" company? Or had she already modified her accent and learnt the manners of a lady by the time she met him? Where did she learn to write so clearly and confidently? How did she learn the French necessary for describing menus and pronouncing them properly to her audience of students and ladies? We can only guess at many of the answers.

If we assume from her absence from her mother's home at the time of the 1871 census that Agnes had left home and was working as a cook's assistant in the kitchen of an affluent family, she would still be classified as working class at that time. She would have benefited from some elementary education so she would already be able to read and write. Being an intelligent woman, she might have "improved" herself by reading books and magazines, and by teaching herself how to write for a more sophisticated readership.

If Agnes worked abroad in her early twenties and had, as Alfred put it, "practised at Paris and Vienna under celebrated chefs",[238] there is no doubt where she learnt French and acquired her considerable culinary skills. In his essay published in *Petits Propos Culinaires*, Jenkins pours scorn on the idea that Agnes ever travelled abroad or studied under prestigious chefs. He suggests that she was either a student at, or was employed by, the Lavenue School of Cookery (which she and Alfred later purchased) and learnt her skills there.[239] However, it is possible that she did indeed travel to Europe and learnt high-class cookery and French there – not independently, but in her capacity as a cook travelling with, and encouraged by, her employer. Unfortunately, we have no idea which of these scenarios (if any) is true.

Powell's emphasis on Henry Irving's rise in social status is that not only did he learn how to speak like a gentleman, but also how to modify his behaviour and bodily movements so that they mirrored those of the higher classes to which he aspired. Even so, he was not entirely accepted as an equal in polite company and suffered some social anxiety as a result. Would that have been the same for Agnes Marshall? I think not. Her hugely successful public demonstrations indicate that she was not lacking in self-confidence. Her natural gracefulness, described in so many reports of her public cooking demonstrations, would have served her well. She clearly had no difficulty in transforming her accent and manner of speech to be accepted as a lady. Key to her success in business, Agnes would have had an innate empathy for the young women training to be cooks. Yet, more importantly, she would have belonged to the same social stratum as the cooks' employers so she would have been able to socialise with them as an equal. How she coped with social interaction with the "upper ten" (the nation's elite) is more uncertain, but it does not seem to have impeded her relationship with someone as near to the top of the social scale as Princess Christian.

Was Mrs Marshall the new Mrs Beeton?

Agnes Marshall was only a young girl when Isabella Beeton died in February 1865. Contrary to the popular image of Isabella Beeton as being "a small tub-like lady in black – rather severe of aspect, strongly resembling Queen Victoria",[240] she was in fact a fashionable young woman of twenty-eight when she died. A rare photograph from 1860 shows Isabella (aged twenty-four) to be "slender" and "elegant", according to her biographer Kathryn Hughes.[241] In this respect, Beeton and Marshall were quite similar. Agnes Marshall was described in an obituary as "a pretty woman […] her figure was slight and graceful".[242] The two women had that much in common; in other respects, their lives were significantly different.

Hughes tell us that Isabella's father, Benjamin Mayson, was a successful cloth merchant with a warehouse and living accommodation in the City of London. Agnes was born to a single mother who later married a cabinet maker. Her mother and stepfather lived in the working-class area of Shoreditch. Isabella too acquired a stepfather, Henry Dorling, at the age of seven. However, Dorling was no cabinet maker; he owned a printing business and was the principal leaseholder of the Grandstand at Epsom racecourse. The Mayson and Dorling children, now united as one family by the marriage of their widowed parents, grew up in a fine house near the racecourse. The young Agnes would also have lived with her half-brother and sisters for a few years before she went into service as a cook's assistant in her teens. When Isabella was fifteen, she was sent to a boarding school at Heidelberg in Germany to finish her education. Unfortunately, we know nothing about Agnes's education or even whether she had any secondary schooling.

While a student in Heidelberg, Isabella developed a passion for baking, which she continued to pursue on her return to Epsom. Hughes points out that making fancy cakes was "one branch of cookery that gentlewomen had traditionally practised". Isabella would certainly not have been learning how to "peel potatoes or cook stew" which would have been socially unacceptable for the daughter of a middle-class household.[243] At the same phase in her life, Agnes was learning her cookery skills (including, we must assume, peeling potatoes and making stew) from "practical training and lessons, through several years, from leading English and Continental authorities" and building on her "home experience [from] earlier than I can well recall".[244]

When Isabella Mayson married Samuel Beeton in 1856, she had no experience of running a household and "didn't know the first thing about cookery" (except, that is, for baking fancy cakes).[245] So how is it that, only five years later, the newly named Mrs Beeton had written what is probably the most famous cookery book in the English language?

Samuel Beeton was a publisher who had launched, among other titles, a magazine called the *Englishwoman's Domestic Magazine*. Soon after they were married, Isabella began to write a column for the publication called "Cooking, Pickling and Preserving", even though she had precious little experience of any of the three.[246] She also wrote the column on women's fashion and was credited as being the "Editress" of the magazine (alongside Samuel as Editor).[247] At its launch, the editor of *The Table* was stated to be Agnes although it is likely that she and Alfred shared the editorship until the magazine's reorganisation in June 1887 when Alfred took sole charge. Agnes was writing about dining and cookery rather than fashion, and her recipes appeared in their own pages right from the first issue of *The Table* and continued until her death, long after her first cookery book was published.

Isabella's recipe column petered out when she began writing her cookery book.[248]

After Isabella had settled into her role as a journalist for the *Englishwoman's Domestic Magazine*, Samuel came up with an even more ambitious project for her. She would write a cookery book. Samuel had published several titles on a wide range of subjects, such as *Beeton's Book of Birds* and *Beeton's Book of Songs*, but the new book would be titled *Beeton's Book of Household Management*. Isabella rose to the challenge, but she approached the project as an editor rather than as a cookery writer. She created hardly any of the recipes in the book herself and probably tested only a small percentage of them in her own kitchen. Hughes reveals that "it is true to say that there is no sentence in the *Book of Household Management* that isn't a tweak or copy of someone else's work".[249]

Isabella's first task was to source enough recipes to fill a complete book. Since she had no recipes of her own, Isabella started out by inviting the readers of the *Englishwoman's Domestic Magazine* to submit their favourite recipes for publication in the journal. When she realised that the recipes which had been submitted would nowhere near fill a book, she followed what was a common practice at the time: lifting the recipes from other cookery books, changing them a little, and claiming them as her own.[250] In particular, Beeton borrowed heavily from Eliza Acton's book from 1845: *Modern Cookery for Private Families*. Agnes Marshall, on the other hand, was a trained and innovative cook who had no need to copy other people's recipes (although very little in the culinary world is ever totally original). She proudly created and tested all her recipes herself and even added a copyright notice to her cookery books stating that "Infringements of copyright will be prosecuted". A similar notice appeared under her recipe column in *The Table*. As we have seen, Agnes had been teaching cookery at her eponymous school for five years before *Mrs. A. B. Marshall's Cookery Book* was published, and she had been writing recipes for publication in *The Table* for two years before that; Isabella had no such experience.

Not only were Agnes and Isabella's books written from different perspectives, but they were published in different ways. *Mrs. A. B. Marshall's Cookery Book* (her most successful book) was first published in 1888 as a stand-alone volume and was priced at five shillings. As we have seen, a new and enlarged edition was published in 1895 at the same price. It contained the entire contents of the first edition plus over one hundred extra recipes and fifty-five additional illustrations. *Beeton's Book of Household Management* was initially published as twenty-four monthly instalments beginning in November 1859. The complete edition of the book, a compendium of all the various instalments, was published in 1861 and was priced at seven shillings and sixpence. The frontispiece of the first edition tells us that the book was "Edited by Mrs Isabella Beeton".[251] Furthermore, cut-down editions of the book appeared in subsequent years – omitting the sections of household management to concentrate solely on the increasingly popular recipes. The titles were *The Englishwoman's Cookery Book*, selling at one shilling, and the more detailed *Dictionary of Every-day Cookery*, priced at three shillings and sixpence. Hughes tells us that, sadly, the Preface to the *Dictionary* was one of the last things that Isabella wrote before she died.[252]

Beeton's Book of Household Management was, as the name suggests, not simply a recipe book. It was, in effect, a complete handbook on how to run a middle-class Victorian household. The book includes chapters on such matters as the role of the mistress of the house, how she should manage the servants in her employment, and how she should organise the kitchen and keep tabs on expenditure. *Mrs. A. B. Marshall's Cookery Book* is primarily a cookery book. The chapters which do not contain recipes are concerned with topics such as "The Art of Dinner

Giving", how to plan a menu, and tips on what to look for (or avoid) when buying ingredients for the recipes.

Both books sold well during their respective authors' lifetimes. *Mrs. A. B. Marshall's Cookery Book* had sold 55,000 by the time of Agnes's death. Hughes tells us that Samuel Beeton claimed that 60,000 copies of *Beeton's Book of Household Management* were sold in the first year of publication alone.[253] However, the fate of the two cookery books could not have been more different. A further 20,000 copies of the enlarged edition of *Mrs. A. B. Marshall's Cookery Book* were published by Simpkin, Marshall, Hamilton, Kent & Co. after Agnes's death. Sometime in the late 1910s, the copyright to the book was sold to the publisher Ward, Lock & Co. It published its own edition, but the book was subsequently discontinued. Ward Lock played a far more significant role in the publication of *Beeton's Book of Household Management*. After Isabella's death, Samuel Beeton continued to publish the book himself; that is, until disaster struck. In 1866, Samuel's financial affairs descended into a perilous state. To avoid formal bankruptcy, he sold the rights to all his publications to Ward, Lock & Tyler (as Ward Lock & Co. was known at the time).[254] From then on, *Mrs. Beeton's Book of Household Management*, now with its modified title, and the "Mrs Beeton" name would be promoted aggressively by Ward Lock until it became the world-renowned literary franchise that we know today.

Agnes Marshall and Isabella Beeton had very different lives. Agnes was an affluent businesswoman and celebrity cook at the time of her death. Isabella was a young journalist with a successful book to her name. The fact that Mrs Beeton's name is still universally known, and that Mrs Marshall's is hardly remembered these days is largely due to Samuel Beeton's financial troubles and the purchase of his book titles by Ward Lock. In many ways, Agnes Marshall is more the successor to Eliza Acton than to Isabella Beeton. Both Agnes and Eliza created and tested their recipes themselves, both were passionate about cooking, and both have been overshadowed in culinary history by Mrs Beeton.

Ice and Ice Cream

In the days before electric-powered refrigeration, the only way to freeze food or keep it cool was to use ice. But if it was a hot summer's day in England and you wanted to chill your champagne, how would you conjure up some ice? The owners of large country estates had been making use of small ice houses for centuries. They would harvest ice from lakes and ponds on their estate in winter and store it in underground or semi-underground ice houses where it might stay frozen for months if enough ice was packed in tightly and the ice house was sufficiently well insulated.

The growing demand for ice in towns and cities in the mid-nineteenth century meant that a more industrial approach was needed to supply sufficient quantities. One of the first entrepreneurs to spot an opening in the market was a Swiss-Italian immigrant by the name of Carlo Gatti. In her book *Coffee and Ices – The Story of Carlo Gatti in London*, Felicity Kinross explains that Gatti had arrived in London from his previous home in Paris in 1847. At first, he sold coffee and hot chestnuts on the streets and lived in a notorious slum area of London, originally known as "The Rookery" because of the intense overcrowding (and, incidentally, the setting for Fagin's den in Charles Dickens' *Oliver Twist*). By the time Carlo Gatti arrived there, the area had been colonised by poor Italian immigrants and had become known as "Little Italy". London in the mid-1800s was a place of stark contrasts: Little Italy, with its poverty, overcrowding and stinking streets, was right next door to the fine houses of Hatton Garden and Ely Place in Holborn.[255]

Gatti was a resourceful and energetic man. He did not remain in a state of poverty for long. Kinross tells us that, in 1849, Gatti joined in partnership with a Swiss chocolatier named Batista Bolla. Gatti then moved with his wife and children from the tenements of

Little Italy to live over the shop in Holborn Hill, alongside Bolla and his family. The pair transformed the premises into a café-restaurant while still keeping it operating as a chocolate factory. Most importantly, as far as Gatti's future career is concerned, Kinross tells us that 129 Holborn Hill had a large cellar where ice could be stored in bulk (in the same way that the Italian-speaking Swiss would have done in their home country). It is likely that Gatti and Bolla began to sell ice cream in the café as was the fashion in Parisian cafés at that time.[256]

Carlo Gatti's businesses grew at an accelerating rate. In 1851 he was operating from two locations in the newly built Hungerford Market, and, by 1853, he had added a further three shops and a café to his properties in the market. Kinross tells us that Gatti's café was modelled on the lines of French cafés and that it was "an entirely new venue for a new type of customer, which included families".[257] His shops were selling confectionery and cakes, penny ice creams, waffles, cold soft drinks and hot coffee.[258]

Research by the London Canal Museum reveals that Gatti had negotiated a licence to cut ice from the Regent's Canal in the early 1850s, although it is uncertain where he stored the ice.[259] The situation becomes clearer later in the decade by which time Gatti is confirmed in the records as being an ice merchant with stores located in Hungerford Market and at New Wharf Road, Islington. New Wharf Road runs along the eastern side of the Battlebridge Basin of the Regent's Canal, and Gatti built two huge ice wells there, the first in 1857 and the second in 1862. The ice wells are still in existence today, although not in use, and are now home to the London Canal Museum. The brick-lined ice wells are each about 30 feet in diameter and 42 feet deep. The sheer bulk of the ice and the efficient design of the ice wells was sufficient to ensure that the ice lost only about a quarter of its weight through melting from the time it was cut in Norway until it was delivered to Gatti's customers.[260]

Ice cut from the Regent's Canal must have been of the poorest quality. It would have suffered from an unreliable supply, except in the coldest winters, and would be unimaginably polluted from surface run-off (although the ice was not intended for direct human consumption but for cooling other foodstuffs). Therefore, it is no surprise that Gatti soon found a more reliable and purer source of ice for his new business. Kinross describes a business letter from 1857 recording that Gatti bought 400 tons – an entire shipload – of ice from a dealer in Norway.[261] The ice ship would have sailed up the River Thames in springtime to the Limehouse Dock where the huge ice blocks would be transferred to canal barges. The barges were then pulled by horses along the Regent's Canal as far as Gatti's new ice well in the Battlebridge Basin. The ice was then unloaded and stored until the following spring when a new shipment arrived from Norway. Carlo Gatti became one of the largest ice merchants in London and, at the peak of the trade, operated more than sixty carts delivering blocks of ice to caterers, ice cream makers, fishmongers, butchers and other businesses across London.

The writer Margaret Visser has suggested that Gatti employed Italian vendors to hawk his carts around London selling penny ice creams.[262] Kinross thinks it is likely, but admits that she has no evidence to support the claim.[263] Street sellers of ice creams became popular in the latter part of Gatti's career, after he had established his continental-style cafés. So whether he did engage in the downmarket business of selling ice creams on the streets is far from certain.

The journalist Henry Mayhew made an extensive survey of the working class in London and published the results of his investigations in 1861–1862 under the title of *London Labour and the London Poor*. Many trades and occupations are chronicled in the book, but the section titled "Of the Street-Sellers of Ices and of Ice Creams" is relatively brief. The reason for the brevity was,

Mayhew tells us, that "The sale of ice-creams was unknown in the streets until last summer, and was first introduced, as a matter of speculation, by a man who was acquainted with the confectionary [sic] business, and who purchased his ices of a confectioner in Holborn".[264] Kinross speculates that the "confectioner in Holborn" might have been Gatti himself.[265] One of the street vendors whom Mayhew interviewed was dubious about ice creams ever becoming popular with London's working class. He told Mayhew:

> Yes, sir, I mind very well the first time I ever sold ices. I don't think they'll ever take greatly in the streets, but there's no saying. Lord! how I've seen the people splutter when they've tasted them for the first time. I did as much myself. They get among the teeth and make you feel as if you tooth-ached all over. I sold mostly strawberry ices. I haven't an idea how they're made, but it's a most wonderful thing in summer – freezing fruits in that way.[266]

He mentions that the customers who enjoyed his ice creams the most were the "servant maids". He suspects that the young women had already got a taste for ice cream "on the sly" from eating a portion of the ices being made for their employers.

However, the pioneer ice cream seller interviewed by Mayhew was wrong about the poor future of selling ices on the streets. By 1872, when Gustave Doré, an artist, and Blanchard Jerrold, a journalist, published *London: a Pilgrimage*, the fashion for eating ice cream among the established middle classes living in the affluent areas of London had already spread to the poorer districts. Jerrold writes:

> It has established penny ices – for which the juvenile population exhibit astonishing voracity – in all the poor districts of the Metropolis. Wherever we have travelled in crowded places of the working population, we have found the

penny ice-man doing a brisk trade – even when his little customers were blue with the cold. The popular ice-vendor is the fashionable rival of the ginger-beer hawker – an old, familiar London figure.[267]

The rapidly increasing popularity of cheap "penny ices" was primarily due to the industry of self-employed Italian ice cream sellers. Most of the ice cream vendors lived in the Saffron Hill area of Little Italy. The campaigning journalist Adolphe Smith and photographer John Thomson interviewed and took photographs of street sellers in London. They published their findings in 1877 as *Street Life in London*. The chapter titled "Halfpenny Ices" tells the Italians' story. They started their day at about 4 a.m. when the men would go off to buy supplies of milk from "little villainous looking and dirty shops" and ice from merchants like Carlo Gatti who, by this time, enjoyed a virtual monopoly of trade with the Italian ice cream sellers.[268] After buying their supplies, they would return to their homes, which doubled up as workshops, to start mixing and then freezing the ice cream. Smith describes the comings and goings of the ice cream sellers:

> Gradually the freezing process is terminated, and then the men, after dressing themselves in a comparatively-speaking decent manner, start off, one by one, to their respective destinations. It is a veritable exodus. The quarter, at first so noisy and full of bustle, is soon deserted […][269]

He continues:

> From this centre the men radiate to all parts of London and the suburbs, many preferring to walk ten and twenty miles per day, to living nearer their "pitch," but further away from their countrymen.[270]

And when their day is done:

> Towards evening, about seven o'clock, the ice-men begin to return. From all points of the compass they approach Saffron Hill. At first there are only one or two to be seen, then, as night draws near, the numbers increase, till their barrows jostle together, and they can hardly pass along.[271]

Smith admires the work ethic and sobriety of the Italians, but is cautious about the quality of their product. He reveals that their "raspberry" ice cream is nothing more than milk and sugar coloured with cochineal and remarks that "This ice is, therefore, a very questionable article, and the less consumed the better the consumer will find himself."[272]

The Italian ice cream vendors sold what were known as "penny licks", although halfpenny sizes were more commonly sold. They would use a wooden spoon to scoop out a portion of ice cream from the container in their cart and slide it into a glass cup known as a "licking glass". The cups looked as if they held a large amount of ice cream, but in fact the glass was very thick and the bowl holding the ice cream very small. The vendor would add to the illusion by sculpting a thin wave of ice cream on the top to make it look taller and the volume appear larger than it really was. The customer would eat the ice cream directly from the licking glass.

The Italians became an integral part of London street life. Andrew Tuer, in his famous book *Old London Street Cries*, writes in 1885:

> The buyers of the so-called penny ices sold in the London streets during the summer months are charged only a halfpenny; and the numerous vendors, usually Italians, need no cry; for the street *gamins*[273] and errand boys buzz around their barrows like flies about a sugar barrel. For obvious

reasons, spoons are not lent. The soft and half-frozen delicacy
is consumed by the combined aid of tongue and fingers.[274]

Tuer's contemporary account contradicts the claim by Kinross,[275] Visser[276] and others that the penny lick vendors were known as "hokey pokey men". Tuer emphasises that the Italians were so well known that they needed no street cry. He does mention hokey pokey, both as a street cry and as a type of ice cream, but remarks (in 1885) that it had appeared on the streets only recently. We know from Jerrold that the penny licks of the Italians had been sold from their carts since at least the early 1870s. Tuer writes:

> Particoloured Neapolitan ices, vended by unmistakable natives of Whitechapel or the New Cut, whose curious cry of "Okey Pokey" originated no one knows how, have lately appeared in the streets. Hokey Pokey is of a firmer make and probably stiffer material than the penny ice of the Italians, which it rivals in public favour; and it is built up of variously flavoured layers. Sold in halfpenny and also penny paper-covered squares, kept until wanted in a circular metal refrigerating pot surrounded by broken ice, Hokey Pokey has the advantage over its rival eaten from glasses, inasmuch as it can be carried away by the purchaser and consumed at leisure. Besides being variously flavoured, Hokey Pokey is dreadfully sweet, dreadfully cold, and hard as a brick. It is whispered that the not unwholesome Swede turnip, crushed into pulp, has been known to form its base, in lieu of more expensive supplies from the cow, whose complex elaboration of cream from turnips is thus unceremoniously abridged.[277]

Visser suggests that the name hokey pokey was an English corruption of the Italian sellers' street cry of "Gelati, ecco un poco!" and other modern writers seem to have used her as a source.[278] However, Robin Weir maintains that the Italian penny lick sellers were known as "Jacks".[279] He suggests that the Italian derivation for the name hokey pokey is "apocryphal" and speculates that it may be the product of some form of Cockney rhyming slang.[280]

Hokey pokey – the ice cream, as opposed to the derivation of the name and the nationality of its sellers – is much better documented. It was made as a block of multi-layered ice cream so it needed a different method of manufacture from the semi-soft penny licks. Penny lick ice cream could be made by hand, or by using a standard machine with a hand-cranked paddle inside a container surrounded by ice and salt (like a more rudimentary version of Marshall's patented machine). Hokey pokey was made by pouring different flavoured and coloured layers, one after the other, into a rectangular tin mould. A lid was then sealed onto the mould with animal fat and the whole assembly immersed in an ice and salt mixture. Weir points out that the texture of the ice cream would be quite coarse due to the large ice crystals which would develop because the ice cream was not churned while it was being frozen. Once frozen, the multi-layered block of ice cream would be released from its mould and cut into individual portions, either penny-sized or halfpenny-sized, and each portion wrapped in waxed paper.[281]

As Tuer points out, hokey pokey had the advantage that it could be taken away and eaten because it was sold in its own wrapper whereas penny licks had to be consumed on the spot. Unfortunately, that gave penny licks another, more serious, disadvantage. Once the customer had eaten the ice cream, they handed the licking glass back to the vendor. The vendor would then rinse out the glass in a bowl of water in his cart and give it a cursory wipe with a cloth. The likelihood that pathogens could be transferred from one customer to another via the unhygienic glasses is evident – the same water was used all day and probably the same cloth too. Penny licks were regularly condemned as a public health hazard by the medical establishment at the time. The report of the Medical Officer of Health for Bethnal Green for 1895 highlights the areas of concern:

> There appear to be four main sources of contamination –
>
> 1. The insanitary condition and filthy surroundings of the premises in which the manufacture is carried on.
>
> 2. Unclean vessels, or the careless admixture of the rough impure ice in the tub with the contents of the cylinder while the process of freezing is going on.
>
> 3. The uncleanly habits of the venders [sic], who have been frequently seen to wipe their sweaty bodies with the towel provided for the glasses.
>
> 4. The method of sale, or rather of serving the cream, from shallow glasses, out of which it is licked; these glasses are sometimes washed after use in the filthy water previously spoken of, but more often they are simply refilled with cream just as they are left by the tongues of the little purchasers, and if the children happen to be convalescent from scarlet fever or diphtheria, the germs of infectious diseases may easily be transferred from one child to another.[282]

However, it was not only the street sellers of ice cream that the health authorities were concerned about. Even the ice creams of the best confectioners in London were not as hygienic as they might be. The annual report of the Medical Officer of Health to the London County Council for 1898 makes interesting reading:

> Dr. Nield Cook then explains that he found about five million microbes per cubic centimetre in samples of Italian ice-cream, and that it occurred to him that it was "desirable to ascertain the bacteriological conditions of the best ice-cream procurable to give a standard for comparison." A sample was

> accordingly purchased at the shop of a "well known west-end confectioner" and subject to precautions detailed by Dr. Cook in his paper, removed to the laboratory and examined.
>
> The result was "contrary to what one would naturally expect," inasmuch as the west-end sample contained the larger number of microbes. [...] Dr. Nield Cook concludes "this much however is certain, that if street ices are to be condemned, we are not justified in condemning them on account of the number or species of bacteria contained in them, for in these respects they are no worse than the best ices sold in the west-end of London."[283]

Quite which "well known west-end confectioner" had their ice cream analysed for bacteria by Dr Cook is unknown; the good doctor was discreet enough not to name the business. The most well-known confectioner in London in 1898 was arguably Gunter's in Berkeley Square who were "Confectioners to Her Majesty" and whose ice creams had been legendary for several decades. Alternatively, the well-known confectioner might have been one of the establishments run by the extended family of Carlo Gatti. Carlo had died in 1878, but his nephews, Agostino and Stephano, ran the upmarket Refreshment Rooms at the Royal Adelaide Gallery on the Strand.

Carlo Gatti expanded his ice trade during his lifetime to become one of the largest ice dealers in London. His ice business continued to thrive even after his death. Kinross tell us that the Carlo Gatti Company merged with two other ice companies in 1901 to become United Carlo Gatti, Stevenson and Slaters Company which continued trading until 1981.[284] The impetus for the amalgamation of three top ice importers was due in part to growing competition from artificial ice manufacturers. Not only that, but the demand for ice was increasing exponentially, and supplies of natural ice from Norway were not always sufficient to satisfy that demand. An article in *The Table*, written during the hot summer of 1900, bemoans the fact that ice had become a scarce commodity. The correspondent complains that the seaside hotel in which they were staying had suffered a "regular ice-famine" and that their ice-puddings and ices were being served "in a semi-frozen condition".[285]

In contrast to the simple ices of the street sellers, the ice creams of the middle classes were becoming more elaborate and *de rigueur* for a sophisticated dinner party. Agnes Marshall's second book on ices, *Fancy Ices* from 1894, reflects this trend. Marshall describes her book as a "fuller treatise on more elaborate styles of service".[286] The only recipes in the book which do not require the frozen mixture to be shaped in a mould are her sorbets or "iced-drinks" which are semi-frozen. Advertisements for Marshall's extensive range of moulds appear in the appendices to the book – there are moulds shaped as castles, beehives, rose baskets and numerous other fancy shapes, including the most elaborate prancing horse. The catalogue exhibits some smaller moulds shaped like various fruits for use as garnishes to the centrepiece. Marshall's fancy ices were not just meant to taste good; they were intended to impress the guests at a dinner party.

One of the most impressive ice creams in the book is Agnes Marshall's "Torpedo Ice". One newspaper reviewer, who had seen Agnes make her creation some years earlier, excitedly claimed that it was "a very amusing sensation for a dinner party".[287] The recipe requires a portion of vanilla custard and a portion of Maraschino custard (both recipes appeared in Marshall's first book, *The Book of Ices*). Each custard is mixed with various dried fruits and fruit purées, and frozen separately. When frozen, the custards are arranged in alternate layers on a platter, and placed in an ice cave to keep cool. Before taking the finished piece to the table, rum is poured into little pockets of tangerine peel arranged around the display and set alight.[288] The result was that the Torpedo Ice "emits a purple flame, which illuminates the whole room […] the effect is very pretty".²⁸⁹ This would surely not fail to impress the diners sitting around the table. What the street urchins would make of it is anybody's guess.

The Servant Question

(This is a revised version of a chapter titled "The Servant Problem" from my book *The Cooking Colonel of Madras* – see: Further Reading)

According to Hugh McLeod "The best index of middle class status in Victorian England was the keeping of a servant, since any middle class man shrank [...] from reducing his wife to the level of a drudge".[290] Few of the growing army of lower middle-class clerks would have been able to afford to employ servants, but no established middle-class family would want the mistress of the house to be seen to be doing the housework or working in the kitchen.

If you browse through late Victorian and Edwardian newspapers and periodicals, you cannot help but notice a recurring reference to what was called "the servant question" in Britain. The problem was twofold – as the middle classes grew in number, there was an increased demand for servants, but there was also a serious lack of training and experience among the servant population.

A book published in 1899, titled *The Servant Problem: An Attempt at Its Solution*, explains the issue in some detail. The author, known only by her pseudonym of "Amara Veritas" (which roughly translates from the Latin as "harsh reality"), describes herself as "an Experienced Mistress". The statistical validity of her sample of correspondents is questionable because she seems to have canvassed her friends, but she does provide some graphic examples of people's unfortunate experiences with their servants. One of her correspondents replies:

> You used to say "I did not know I was born" in regard to the "Servant Question". I do now. I have a cook who sometimes sends up part of the dinner and forgets the other half; one day she forgot it altogether. When gently remonstrated with, she

said: "I didn't come 'ere to kill myself with your work. I came becos I 'eard it was an easy place, and plenty of good livin'." My house is just filthy [...] and I dare not say a word, else they will just rise and walk out.[291]

Another reported:

> I dare not say anything is wrong, in case I receive notice on the spot – and I might get worse, or none at all; I therefore put up with an otherwise almost intolerable state of matters.[292]

And yet another: "We live in a state of perpetual fermentation and unrest through them, not knowing what the next minute may bring forth." One lamented: "They have been more than anything else the cause of angry words between my husband and myself in our married life."[293]

The servant problem caught Colonel Kenney-Herbert off guard on his return to England on furlough in 1876. He tackles the topic in one of his articles from London for the Madras newspaper, *The Athenaeum and Daily News*. Before he left India, Kenney-Herbert had been told by a friend who had just returned from London: "Wait till you have had a little experience of London servants." He soon gains some unwelcome personal experience of what she meant:

> I little thought at the moment that my experience would, in a short space of time, be so extensive, and so bitter. In a year we have had a deaf cook, a cook blind of one eye, two drunken cooks, an eccentric cook, and a very amorous cook. All these persons started satisfactorily; their failings were discovered as acquaintance ripened into intimacy. We have only had one utterly incompetent cook whose method of cooking macaroni with cheese deserves to be recorded; she put it, without any previous soaking or boiling, hard and dry into the oven on the top of some thick slices of cheese. Have you ever tried to bite

a pipe of macaroni *au natural*, and found it a little harder than wood? Well, if you bake it you can get it still harder – a capital thing to snap a tooth upon. This unhappy woman once made a pie the paste of which looked like the cover of an old parish register, and so hard that no knife could penetrate it.[294]

Drunken cooks, like the one in Kenney-Herbert's example, seem to have been all too common. However, Amara Veritas does have some sympathy with their plight:

> Have ladies and gentlemen, who have their refreshing baths every morning, their round of outdoor exercises and pleasures daily, ever thought what it must mean to stand all day in a hot kitchen, over a broiling fire, and this, week in, week out, with hardly any intermission?
>
> Certainly it must be a most trying life, and one that entails a strain on the worker's vitality. It can scarcely, then, be a matter of wonder that so many cooks fall victims to that terrible craving for strong drink – a failing that has caused their name and their profession to be quite a byword.[295]

Amara Veritas speaks from personal experience, telling of a cook in her employ who would often be drunk by midday, and who would boast to her fellow servants about how much alcohol she could consume. The servants begged their mistress to sack the cook because they could not stand the disruption any longer, having to do extra work to cover for her when she was incapacitated. When the cook was finally dismissed, the housemaid found bottles of spirits stashed around the house in the most unlikely of places, including up the chimney!

The discussion was not all one-sided. In her book, *Servants' Stories*, Michelle Higgs tells the story of domestic service from the employees' point of view. A domestic servant's day was long and the work hard. Servants frequently wrote to local newspapers about the harsh conditions under which they had to work. One wrote to the *Western Mail* in November 1892 complaining:

> No one seems to heed our long hours or our holidays, which are (like angels' visits) few and far between. There seems no other class working at a greater disadvantage. For instance, no servant can expect a situation who had not got a good reference and a long one from where she last lived. It often happens she has been living with unprincipled people, who think not half so much of their servants as they do of their dumb animals. What is it to them if the girl does not get a situation?[296]

It is noticeable from reading the young woman's letter how well educated she was. By 1892, working-class girls were beginning to enjoy a longer period of education. In some ways, this made the "servant problem" even worse. The brighter ones might choose teaching, nursing or clerical work. Others opted for employment which involved more regular hours and increased leisure time, such as shop or factory work. However, domestic servants had the advantage of having their board and lodging paid by their employers; advertisements for positions usually included the words "all found" in addition to the remuneration being offered. The disadvantage of taking shop or factory work was that the young person would need to pay for their food and lodging out of their own wages.

Amara Veritas claims that the servant problem was one that affected nearly every home (by which she means middle- and upper-class homes). She explains that the demand for servants was far greater than the supply: this created a situation where servants could almost do as they pleased or, if reprimanded, walk out and easily find another job. She points out that if her husband had a vacancy for a clerk, he would place an advertisement in the newspaper and be inundated with applications. However, if she had a vacancy for a cook or a housemaid, she would have to take whomever she could get, and on whatever terms they demanded.

Looking at the question from the servants' side, their employment was highly insecure. There was no contract of employment, and the mistress of the house could sack a servant with no notice even for a slight misdemeanour. The rules of the house were often strict. Eliza Lynn Linton wrote about housemaids in 1874, commenting that they were allowed "no followers [boyfriends], no friends in the kitchen, no laughing to be heard above stairs."[297] Cooks and housemaids tended to change their jobs frequently in the hope that it might provide them with a more hospitable working environment or better pay and conditions.

Apart from placing an advertisement in the newspapers, the other common way to find domestic servants was through registry offices (what we would now call employment agencies). There seems to have been a quite a few agencies that engaged in dubious practices, at least in the experience of Amara Veritas and her acquaintances. She explains that the registry office would demand a fee from the prospective employer before they would even consider suggesting suitable servants. The fee was non-returnable and did not guarantee that the agency would find appropriate staff or even if they had any servants on their books at the time.

Amara Veritas gives examples of popular scams undertaken by the less scrupulous agencies. One of the most common tricks played by the registry offices was to place an advertisement in the newspapers claiming that it had several experienced cooks on its books who had glowing references from previous employers. The response was that numerous ladies, desperate to find a reliable cook, would visit the agency, pay a fee just to be "on the books" and interview the applicants. The problem was that there was only one cook, and it was she who was interviewing the ladies rather than vice versa while calculating which prospective mistress would agree to the most advantageous benefits. The lucky lady who reluctantly gave in to the cook's demands then had the honour of paying the agency a second fee once she employed the cook. The other disappointed ladies would go home empty-handed, but still having parted with the initial fee.[298]

Kenney-Herbert had his own bad experiences of the registry offices that he had to use while looking for servants during his furlough in London:

> There can be no doubt that there is the utmost difficulty experienced by people whose stay in London is limited to a year or so, in procuring servants of a superior class, for the riff-raff one has to select from at the Registry Offices is, as a rule quite worthless.[299]

However, not all the registry offices engaged in sharp practices, and even Amara Veritas concedes that some of the agencies, especially the smaller ones, provided a good service. She remarks on an advertisement that she had seen in a newspaper for the sale of a registry office, which reads:

> Agency to be disposed of.
> Easily worked.
> Handsome profits.
> Best principles.[300]

She is outraged that if an agency working on the best principles could still make a handsome profit, then those who used the underhand methods she describes must be making enormous amounts of money at the expense of desperate ladies.

On Kenney-Herbert's retirement back to England from the Madras Cavalry in 1892, he launched a registry office of his own in conjunction with his new cookery school – The Common-Sense Cookery Association. Marshall's School of Cookery had been training cooks and acting as a reputable recruitment agency for domestic staff since 1883. Marshall's weekly newspaper *The Table* foresaw the crisis coming in the recruitment of domestic servants. An editorial from October 1886 reads:

> Surely, there is a Great Servant Question looming, the effect of which in the near future, unless something is done to stay the increasing gap between supply and demand, and to attract to the domestic ranks the "surplus women" of our population, few can now foresee. That such a gap really and truly does exist is shown by the fact that whilst 6,400 mistresses have applied for cooks at Marshall's School of Cookery during the last two years, only 3,700 cooks have offered themselves for the situations, notwithstanding the fact that single-handed cooks are not charged […] any fee whatever.[301]

The "servant question" not only involved staff shortages, but a lack of training meant that the quality of work was also a significant issue. Many cooks received the limited training they had as a kitchen maid, under the guidance of a cook who might have been poorly trained herself. Others, especially those migrating to the large cites from the countryside, went straight from helping their mothers in the home kitchen to working as a cook for a family, with no formal training whatsoever. Kenney-Herbert identifies the problem in an article he wrote for *The Nineteenth Century* titled, appropriately enough, "The Teaching of Cookery". He cites the opening of the National Training School of Cookery as a landmark in the history of cookery teaching. Prior to that, there had been no significant cookery schools in London, let alone around the country.[302]

The National emerged out of the organisation for the Great Exhibition of 1851. The success of the Great Exhibition led to a series of smaller exhibitions in South Kensington, held on what is now Exhibition Road. Henry Cole – later Sir Henry Cole – was asked to organise the 1873 exhibition and he thought it would be a good idea to include cooking as one of the subjects. Little did he know when he first started planning it just how successful the cookery demonstrations would be. In her seminal work, *The National: The Story of a Pioneer College*, Dorothy Stone tells us that the exhibition committee chose a flamboyant character named John Charles Buckmaster to give the cookery demonstrations. They could not have chosen a better person. The exhibition drew in half a million visitors, and Buckmaster's lectures proved to be a particular hit with the public. Kenney-Herbert notes in his article that Buckmaster gave a running commentary while a team of cooks made the dishes in front of the audience – even Queen Victoria attended one of the demonstrations.

Not only was the exhibition successful, but it also made a profit. Entrance to the cookery exhibition was free (except for the seats in the front row, whose occupants were allowed to taste the dishes), but the committee had wisely taken the decision to sell recipes of the dishes being demonstrated. The audiences could not buy the recipes fast enough, and the cookery exhibition made an astonishing profit of £1,765 (about £152,000 in today's money).[303]

When the exhibition closed, Cole persuaded the committee to establish a permanent training school for cookery. Stone writes of Cole's aims:

> The school was not to fill any purely local need; it was not to be a 'South Kensington', nor even a 'London' school. It was to be a 'National' school in the sense that it was designed to pioneer a national effort for the recognition and teaching of cookery (and incidentally hygiene) as being vital to the interests and the well being of the whole country.[304]

The National opened in March 1874 using the same premises as the previous year's exhibition. The premises and all the equipment from the exhibition were provided free of charge, but the corrugated iron buildings were only designed for temporary use and inevitably caused problems of their own. They were cold in winter, unbearably hot in summer and lacked adequate light and ventilation. The school had to wait until 1889 before it could move into a purpose-built building in Buckingham Palace Road, where it remained for the rest of its existence.

Edith Nicolls, soon to become Mrs Charles Clarke, was appointed Lady Superintendent of The National in 1875. She remained in the job for forty-five years, guiding the school through good times and bad. The learners' classes were the most popular. Ladies were invited to bring their cooks with them to the school; the cooks were encouraged to take written and practical exams, and to gain certificates of competence. New classes were soon introduced, in line with the school's objectives, to train cookery teachers. By the end of the 1870s, graduates from The National had spread throughout the country and were teaching in newly opened cookery schools.

It is interesting to note that students were not restricted by social class or race. Stone refers to a report by Eliza Youmans, who trained at The National and wrote the American edition of the school's handbook. Youmans wrote:

> I was a pupil there for several weeks and carefully observed its operations. The classes showed the most extraordinary mental and social diversity. There were cultivated ladies, the daughters of country gentlemen, old housekeepers, servants, cooks, and coloured girls from South Africa, together with a large proportion of intelligent young women who were preparing to become teachers.[305]

As soon as The National had moved to its permanent home in Buckingham Palace Road, Edith Clarke was able to take full advantage of the enhanced facilities in the new training kitchens, and devised a new curriculum to reflect current educational needs.

She divided the classes into two categories: plain cookery and high-class cookery. Plain cookery was further subdivided into household cookery, for cooks hoping to gain employment in middle-class households, and artisan cookery, for the wives of manual workers and for working-class schoolchildren. Students who wanted to become cookery teachers and gain The National's full Teaching Diploma had to study for and pass exams in both categories.

As we have seen, Agnes Marshall disapproved of the way in which The National was funded and considered it to have an unfair financial advantage over private cookery schools like her own. The National's move to its new premises provoked more criticism in *The Table*.[306] It was to benefit from a lease on the premises, granted by the Duke of Westminster, free of ground rent for the first two years. In addition, the school intended to open a registry office for servants (which would be in direct competition to Marshall's) and a restaurant which would serve meals to the public that had been cooked by its students. *The Table* found the new arrangements to be a "startling departure" from The National's previous constitution and a move away from its stated aim of being a national organisation.

The National had been in competition with numerous rival cookery schools for some time. Advertisements for The National in the London newspapers of 1894 sit right alongside advertisements for Kenney-Herbert's Common-Sense Cookery Association and, of course, Marshall's School of Cookery. The three cookery schools seem to have been in competition to outdo each other with a record of their accomplishments and expertise, but in terms of column inches for the advertisements, Marshall's won hands down.[307]

Agnes Marshall was not overly modest about the achievements of her school, claiming in her advertisements, with some justification, that it was:

"The largest and most successful of its kind in the world."

Online Pictures

There is a special area on The Curry House website for owners of *Agnes Marshall: From Scullery Maid to Victorian Celebrity Cook*. The bonus material includes illustrations from Agnes Marshall's books, Victorian prints and material used in David Smith's research for this book. Please visit:

curryhouse.co.uk/marshall

Publication Dates for Agnes Marshall's Books

Agnes Marshall's books do not usually show a publication date or an edition number. Instead, the various editions are identified by the number of copies printed. An approximate correlation between the thousands of copies printed and the date of publication is set out below.

YEAR	SOURCE	BOOK TITLE & COPIES PRINTED
1885	Advertisement, *Illustrated London News*, 25 July 1885	*The Book of Ices* published
1888	Advertisement, *The Morning Post*, 28 April 1888	*Mrs. A. B. Marshall's Cookery Book* published
1889	Advertisement, *Western Daily Press*, 3 April 1889	*The Book of Ices* – impression not specified *Cookery Book* – tenth thousand
	Advertisement, *The Table*, 19 October 1889	*The Book of Ices* – "fourth edition" *Cookery Book* – impression not specified
1891	Advertisements, *The Morning Post,* February 1891 onwards	*The Book of Ices* – impression not specified

		Cookery Book – fifteenth thousand
	Advertisement, *Liverpool Mercury*, 12 December 1891	*The Book of Ices* – impression not specified *Cookery Book* – twentieth thousand
1892	"New Books", *Dundee Advertiser*, 21 January 1892	*Mrs. A. B. Marshall's Larger Cookery Book* published
1893	Advertisement, *The Table*, 7 January 1893	*The Book of Ices* – sixth thousand *Cookery Book* – twentieth thousand *Larger Cookery Book* – "just out"
	Advertisement, *The Table*, 20 May 1893	*The Book of Ices* – sixth thousand *Cookery Book* – twenty-fifth thousand *Larger Cookery Book* – "just out"
1894	Advertisement, *The Queen*, 24 March 1894	*The Book of Ices* – seventh thousand *Cookery Book* – twenty-fifth thousand *Larger Cookery Book* – fourth thousand

	"Fancy Ices", *The Morning Post*, 20 June 1894	*Fancy Ices* published
1895	"Mrs. A. B. Marshall's Publications", *The Table*, 16 February 1895	*The Book of Ices* – eighth thousand *Cookery Book* – thirtieth thousand *Larger Cookery Book* – fourth thousand *Fancy Ices* – "just published"
	Advertisement, *The Table*, 27 April 1895	Revised and enlarged edition of *Mrs. A. B. Marshall's Cookery Book* published
1896	Advertisement, *The Queen*, 20 June 1896	*The Book of Ices* – impression not specified *Cookery Book* – thirty-fifth thousand *Larger Cookery Book* – sixth thousand *Fancy Ices* – impression not specified
1897	Advertisement, *The Queen*, 3 April 1897	*The Book of Ices* – tenth thousand *Cookery Book* – thirty-fifth thousand *Larger Cookery Book* – sixth thousand

		Fancy Ices – impression not specified
1898	Advertisement, *The Queen*, 18 June 1898	*The Book of Ices* – tenth thousand *Cookery Book* – fortieth thousand *Larger Cookery Book* – sixth thousand *Fancy Ices* – second thousand
1899	Advertisement, *The Queen*, 14 February 1899	*The Book of Ices* – twelfth thousand *Cookery Book* – fortieth thousand *Larger Cookery Book* – seventh thousand *Fancy Ices* – second thousand
1900	Advertisement, *The Table*, 6 January 1900	*The Book of Ices* – twelfth thousand *Cookery Book* – forty-fifth thousand *Larger Cookery Book* – seventh thousand *Fancy Ices* – second thousand
1902	Preface, *Mrs. A. B. Marshall's Larger Cookery Book*, February 1902	*The Book of Ices* – fourteenth thousand *Cookery Book* – fiftieth thousand

		Larger Cookery Book – eighth thousand
*Fancy Ice*s – second thousand
1905	"Books by Mrs. A.B. Marshall", *The Table*, 5 August 1905	*The Book of Ices* – fourteenth thousand
Cookery Book – fifty-fifth thousand
Larger Cookery Book – eighth thousand
Fancy Ices – second thousand
1906	Advertisement, *Illustrated London News*, 1 December 1906	*The Book of Ices* – fifteenth thousand
Cookery Book – sixtieth thousand
Larger Cookery Book – ninth thousand
Fancy Ices – impression not specified
1909	Copy of *Mrs. A. B. Marshall's Cookery Book*, hand-dated 1909	*The Book of Ices* – sixteenth thousand
Cookery Book – sixty-fifth thousand
Larger Cookery Book – ninth thousand
Fancy Ices – third thousand
1912	Advertisement, *The Gentlewoman*, 16 November 1912	*The Book of Ices* – impression not specified

		Cookery Book – sixty-fifth thousand
		Larger Cookery Book – tenth thousand
		Fancy Ices – impression not specified
1913–1918	Advertisement in a late copy of *The Book of Ices*	*The Book of Ices* – twenty-first thousand
		Cookery Book – seventy-fifth thousand

Primary Sources

Marshall, Agnes Bertha, *The Book of Ices* (Marshall's School of Cookery, 1885).

Marshall, Agnes Bertha, *Mrs. A. B. Marshall's Cookery Book* (Simpkin, Marshall, Hamilton, Kent & Co., 1888).

Marshall, Agnes Bertha, *Mrs. A. B. Marshall's Larger Cookery Book of Extra Recipes* (Simpkin, Marshall, Hamilton, Kent & Co., 1892).

Marshall, Agnes Bertha, *Fancy Ices* (Robert Hayes Ltd., 1894).

Marshall, Agnes Bertha (editor), *The Table* (Marshall's School of Cookery, published weekly from 12 June 1886 until 1918).

Doré, Gustave, and Blanchard Jerrold, *London: a Pilgrimage* (Grant & Co., 1872).

Kenney-Herbert, Arthur Robert ("Wyvern"), *Furlough Reminiscences* (Higginbotham & Co., 1880).

Mayhew, Henry, *London Labour and the London Poor* (Griffin, Bohn, and Company, 1861).

Thomson, John, and Adolphe Smith, *Street Life in London* (Sampson Lowe, Marston, Searle, & Rivington, 1877).

Tuer, Andrew W., *Old London Street Cries and the Cries of Today* (Leadenhall Press, 1885).

Veritas, Amara, *The Servant Problem: An Attempt at Its Solution by an Experienced Mistress* (Simpkin, Marshall, Hamilton, Kent & Co. 1899).

Further Reading

Crossick, Geoffrey (editor), *The Lower Middle Class in Britain 1870-1914* (Routledge, 2016).

Higgs, Michelle, *A Visitor's Guide to Victorian England* (Pen & Sword History, 2014).

Higgs, Michelle, *Servants' Stories* (Pen & Sword History, 2015).

Hughes, Kathryn, *The Short Life and Long Times of Mrs Beeton* (Harper Perennial, 2006).

Kinross, Felicity, *Coffee and Ices: The Story of Carlo Gatti in London* (London Canal Museum, second edition, 2020).

Picard, Liza, *Victorian London* (Phoenix, 2006).

Pomeroy, Ralph, *The Ice Cream Connection* (Paddington Press, 1975).

Smith, David W., *The Cooking Colonel of Madras* (Lulu.com, 2018 – revised 2020).

Stone, Dorothy, *The National: The Story of a Pioneer College* (Robert Hale & Company, 1976).

Weir, Robin, Peter Brears, John Deith, and Peter Barham, *Mrs Marshall: The Greatest Victorian Ice Cream Maker* (Smith Settle for Syon House, 1998).

Notes

[1] "A Pretty Luncheon", *The Morning Post*, 17 October 1887.
[2] "A Pretty Luncheon", *The Times*, 17 October 1887. Quoted in: Agnes Bertha Marshall, *Mrs. A. B. Marshall's Cookery Book,* fifteenth thousand (Simpkin, Marshall, Hamilton, Kent & Co., undated, c.1891), Advertisements, 4.
[3] Robin Weir, John Deith, Peter Brears and Peter Barham, *Mrs Marshall: The Greatest Victorian Ice Cream* Maker (Smith Settle for Syon House, 1998), 11–12.
[4] Walthamstow is now in London but was then in the county of Essex.
[5] Terry Jenkins, "The Truth about Mrs Marshall", *Petits Propos Culinaires*, 112 (Prospect Books, November 2018), 100–112.
[6] The censuses of 1881 and 1891.
[7] "Memorial Window", *Uxbridge & West Drayton Gazette*, 11 August 1906.
[8] Now Thurtle Road.
[9] The census record has been transcribed (on FindMyPast.com) to read that John Wells was a "boarder" and was married, but the original record states that he was Charles Wells' brother and was unmarried.
[10] Facsimile of Susan Smith and John Wells' marriage certificate published in "The Truth about Mrs Marshall", *Petits Propos Culinaires*, 112 (Prospect Books, November 2018), 102.
[11] Terry Jenkins, "The Truth about Mrs Marshall", *Petits Propos Culinaires*, 112 (Prospect Books, November 2018), 103.
[12] Now Dysart Street.
[13] "The Maps Descriptive of London Poverty are perhaps the most distinctive product of Charles Booth's Inquiry into Life and Labour in London (1886–1903). An early example of social

cartography, each street is coloured to indicate the income and social class of its inhabitants." Charles Booth's London, LSE, accessed 12 December 2022, https://booth.lse.ac.uk/learn-more/what-were-the-poverty-maps.

[14] Hanover Square is now in London but was then in the county of Middlesex.

[15] "Cookery and Cook-Making, An Interview with Mr. Marshall", *The Pall Mall Gazette*, 14 October 1886.

[16] Agnes Bertha Marshall, *Mrs. A. B. Marshall's Cookery Book,* fifteenth thousand (Simpkin, Marshall, Hamilton, Kent & Co., undated, c.1891), Preface.

[17] "British Orphan Asylum, Clapham, London / Slough, Buckinghamshire", Children's Homes, accessed 7 January 2023, http://www.childrenshomes.org.uk/BritishOrphan/

[18] *Old Bailey Proceedings Online* (www.oldbaileyonline.org), March 1879, trial of Alfred William Marshall (31), t18790331-418.

[19] Calculation made using the Bank of England Inflation Calculator, accessed 9 January 2023, https://www.bankofengland.co.uk/monetary-policy/inflation/inflation-calculator.

[20] *Old Bailey Proceedings Online* (www.oldbaileyonline.org), March 1879, trial of Alfred William Marshall (31), t18790331-418.

[21] *Ibid.*

[22] Robin Weir, John Deith, Peter Brears and Peter Barham, *Mrs Marshall: The Greatest Victorian Ice Cream Maker* (Smith Settle for Syon House, 1998), 13.

[23] Ruth Richardson, "Foundlings, orphans and unmarried mothers", British Library, published 15 May 2014, https://www.bl.uk/romantics-and-victorians/articles/foundlings-orphans-and-unmarried-mothers.

[24] Not 1880 as stated by Deith.
[25] 8 Wellington Road, the house next door to Agnes and Alfred's, sold for £2.5 million in 2021 according to Rightmove, accessed 7 January 2023, https://www.rightmove.co.uk/house-prices/nw8/wellington-road.html.
[26] Advertisement, *London Evening Standard*, 30 June 1883.
[27] There is a misprint in some advertisements naming the cookery school bought by the Marshalls as "Lavenne". However, most advertisements state that the school was named "Lavenue", including those from the "A. M. Lavenue School of Cookery" itself. For example, an advertisement in *The Hour*, 10 September 1873.
[28] Advertisement, *The Morning Post*, 13 November 1883.
[29] "Cookery and Cook-Making, An Interview with Mr. Marshall", *The Pall Mall Gazette*, 14 October 1886.
[30] *Ibid.*
[31] Advertisement, *London Evening Standard*, 25 Aug 1884.
[32] *Ibid.*
[33] "Cookery and Cook-Making, An Interview with Mr. Marshall", *The Pall Mall Gazette*, 14 October 1886.
[34] "You're Dead To Me: The History of Ice Cream", BBC, accessed 23 November 2022, https://www.bbc.co.uk/programmes/articles/5cSf963VtsNDsr3qj0qCVNV/8-scoops-on-the-history-of-ice-cream.
[35] For example, Henrietta Vansittart invented an improved design for a marine screw propeller and obtained a patent in her own name in 1868 – "Women in Engineering", Science Museum, accessed 14 December 2022, https://www.sciencemuseum.org.uk/objects-and-stories/women-engineering.
[36] Robin Weir, John Deith, Peter Brears and Peter Barham, *Mrs Marshall: The Greatest Victorian Ice Cream Maker* (Smith Settle for Syon House, 1998), 3–4.

[37] Agnes Bertha Marshall, *The Book of Ices* (Marshall's School of Cookery, 1885 – twelfth thousand), 56.
[38] Advertisement, *The Table*, 3 July 1886.
[39] One quart is equivalent to two British pints or 1.14 litres.
[40] Agnes Bertha Marshall, *The Book of Ices* (Marshall's School of Cookery, 1885 – twelfth thousand).
[41] Advertisement, *Illustrated London News*, 25 July 1885.
[42] Agnes Bertha Marshall, *The Book of Ices* (Marshall's School of Cookery, 1885 – twelfth thousand), 1–2.
[43] *Ibid.*, 6.
[44] Robin Weir, John Deith, Peter Brears and Peter Barham, *Mrs Marshall: The Greatest Victorian Ice Cream Maker* (Smith Settle for Syon House, 1998), 3.
[45] Advertisement, *The Morning Post*, 26 February 1885.
[46] "Cookery and Cook-Making, An Interview with Mr. Marshall", *The Pall Mall Gazette*, 14 October 1886.
[47] "Contributors to The Table", *The Table*, 14 August 1886.
[48] "To Our Readers", *The Table*, 4 September 1886.
[49] "Table Talk", *The Table*, 23 October 1886.
[50] "Table Talk", *The Table*, 12 June 1886.
[51] "The Table", *Aberdeen People's Journal*, 3 July 1886.
[52] "Cookery", *The Table*, 12 June 1886.
[53] P.O.O. is the abbreviation for a Post Office Order (postal order).
[54] Following the passing of the Married Women's Property Act in 1882, Agnes would have been entitled to open a bank account in her own name, independent of her husband.
[55] "Mr. Marshall", *The Globe*, 15 June 1886.
[56] Calculation made using the Bank of England Inflation Calculator, accessed 9 January 2023, https://www.bankofengland.co.uk/monetary-policy/inflation/inflation-calculator.

[57] Advertisement, *The Morning Post*, 2 May 1885.
[58] "Marshall's School of Cookery", *The Table*, 26 June 1886.
[59] "Programme for Week Commencing Monday July 12, 1886", *The Table*, 10 July 1886.
[60] "Marshall's School of Cookery", *The Table*, 10 July 1886.
[61] La Vieille, "A Visit to a Cooking School", *The Queen*, 6 November 1886.
[62] "Situations Vacant", *The Weekly Dispatch*, London, 17 January 1886; "Situations Vacant", *The Table*, 1 January 1887.
[63] rare, exotic – *Oxford English Dictionary*
[64] La Vieille, "A Visit to a Cooking School", *The Queen*, 6 November 1886.
[65] a metal plate heated and placed over food to brown it – *Oxford English Dictionary*
[66] La Vieille, "A Visit to a Cooking School", *The Queen*, 6 November 1886.
[67] "A Visit to a Cooking School", *The Table*, 13 November 1886.
[68] "Notice", *The Table*, 25 December 1886.
[69] Marshall's School of Cookery advertisement, *The Morning Post*, 10 February 1887.
[70] International School of Cookery advertisement, *The Morning Post*, 10 February 1887.
[71] International School of Cookery advertisement, *The Morning Post*, 3 August 1887.
[72] Marshall's School of Cookery advertisement, *The Morning Post*, 1 August 1887.
[73] Editorial, *The Table*, 17 July 1886.
[74] "Programmes", *The Table*, 9 July 1887.
[75] Supplement, *The Table*, 6 August 1887.
[76] "Mrs. Marshall's Lecture in Birmingham", *The Table*, 13 August 1887.
[77] S., "A 'Whole Dinner' Lesson", *The Queen*, 28 May 1887.

[78] "Programmes", *The Table*, 23 April 1887.
[79] "Programmes", *The Table*, 23 July 1887.
[80] "A Pretty Luncheon", *Cheltenham Examiner*, 19 October 1887.
[81] "A Pretty Luncheon", *The Morning Post*, 17 October 1887.
[82] "A Pretty Luncheon", *Leeds Mercury*, 16 August 1887.
[83] E.A.B, "A Pretty Luncheon", *The Queen*, 22 October 1887.
[84] "Table Talk", *The Table*, 7 January 1888.
[85] Oscar Wilde, "Literary and other Notes", *The Woman's World*, January 1888.
[86] Agnes Bertha Marshall, *Mrs. A. B. Marshall's Cookery Book,* fifteenth thousand (Simpkin, Marshall, Hamilton, Kent & Co., undated, c.1891).
[87] The "Marshall" in the publisher's name was not related to Alfred Marshall, but refers to Richard Marshall, one of the original partners in the firm.
[88] Agnes Bertha Marshall, *Mrs. A. B. Marshall's Cookery Book,* fifteenth thousand (Simpkin, Marshall, Hamilton, Kent & Co., undated, c.1891).
[89] *Ibid.*, 5.
[90] *Ibid.*, 384.
[91] Ian Kelly, *Cooking for Kings: The Life of Antonin Carême, the First Celebrity Chef* (Short Books, 2004), 15.
[92] Agnes Bertha Marshall, *Mrs. A. B. Marshall's Cookery Book,* fifteenth thousand (Simpkin, Marshall, Hamilton, Kent & Co., undated, c.1891), 407.
[93] *Ibid.*, 392.
[94] "Table Talk", *The Table*, 22 September 1888.
[95] "Table Talk", *The Table*, 5 January 1889.
[96] Advertisement, *The Table*, 5 January 1889.
[97] Advertisement, *The Table*, 1 June 1889.
[98] Calculation made using the Bank of England Inflation Calculator, accessed 12 January 2023,

https://www.bankofengland.co.uk/monetary-policy/inflation/inflation-calculator.

[99] "Table Talk", *The Table*, 20 April 1889.

[100] "Table Talk", *The Table*, 4 May 1889.

[101] Agnes Marshall's books do not show a publication date or an edition number. Instead, the various editions are identified by the number of copies printed. In this case, the "Tenth Thousand" was announced in advertisements dating from 1889. See: Publication Dates for Agnes Marshall's Books for an approximate correlation between the number of copies printed and the date.

[102] "Why We Change Our Printers", *The Table*, 1 March 1890.

[103] The National Archives, BT 31/15074/31415: Company No: 31415; Table Newspaper Company Ltd. Incorporated in 1890. Dissolved between 1916 and 1932.

[104] *Ibid.*

[105] "Notice to Subscribers", *The Table*, 10 May 1890.

[106] "N. Ruffin", Advertisement, *The Table*, 10 January 1891.

[107] The Editor, "To Our Readers", *The Table*, 3 May 1890.

[108] "Important Notice", *The Table*, 5 July 1890.

[109] "Marshall's School of Cookery", *The Table*, 3 January 1891.

[110] The National Archives, BT 31/15074/31415: Company No: 31415; Table Newspaper Company Ltd. Incorporated in 1890. Dissolved between 1916 and 1932.

[111] "Notice", *The Table*, 3 October 1891.

[112] "To Our Readers", *The Table*, 7 November 1891.

[113] "Notice", *The Table*, 26 December 1891.

[114] The National Archives, BT 31/15074/31415: Company No: 31415; Table Newspaper Company Ltd. Incorporated in 1890. Dissolved between 1916 and 1932.

[115] Robin Weir, John Deith, Peter Brears and Peter Barham, *Mrs Marshall: The Greatest Victorian Ice Cream Maker* (Smith Settle for Syon House, 1998), 20.
[116] London Metropolitan Archives, City of London, Middlesex Deeds Registry, MDR/1892/012/0001-0250, 181.
[117] *Ibid.*
[118] Terry Jenkins, "The Truth about Mrs Marshall", *Petits Propos Culinaires*, 112 (Prospect Books, November 2018), 111.
[119] "Fatal Accident at Pinner", *Uxbridge & West Drayton Gazette*, 28 July 1894.
[120] Advertisement, *Liverpool Mercury*, 12 December 1891.
[121] Advertisement, *The Morning Post*, 16 November 1891.
[122] "New Books", *Dundee Advertiser*, 21 January 1892.
[123] One guinea is one pound and one shilling, or twenty-one shillings.
[124] Agnes Bertha Marshall, *Mrs. A. B. Marshall's Larger Cookery Book of Extra Recipes,* eighth thousand (Simpkin, Marshall, Hamilton, Kent & Co., Preface dated February 1902).
[125] *Ibid.*
[126] *Ibid.*, 192.
[127] *Ibid.*, 457. Note: the picture is featured on the cover of this book.
[128] "The upper ten" or "upper ten thousand" refers to the elite in society – the upper classes.
[129] "New Books", *Dundee Advertiser*, 21 January 1892.
[130] "Mrs. A. B. Marshall's Larger Cookery Book", *The Queen*, 30 January 1892.
[131] "An Entire Dinner Lesson", *The Queen*, 6 August 1892.
[132] Advertisement, *The Queen*, 13 February 1892.
[133] The exact date of the latest change is unknown. The volume of *The Table* for 1892 is missing from the collection at the British Library.

[134] "A Ball Supper Lesson", *The Queen*, 8 April 1893.
[135] Epicure, "A New Departure in a Cookery Lesson", *The Gentlewoman*, 11 March 1893.
[136] "Ball Supper Lesson", *Leeds Mercury*, 30 March 1893.
[137] "An Introduction to F & C Osler, Glassmakers to the Queen", Nicholas Wells Antiques Ltd., last modified 14 May 2020, https://nicholaswells.com/news/an-introduction-to-f-c-osler-a-brief-history-of-f-c-osler/.
[138] "A Ball Supper Lesson", *The Queen*, 8 April 1893.
[139] Reviews cited in "Our Supplement", *The Table*, 22 April 1893.
[140] Diner Out, "Across the Table", *The Table*, 9 April 1898.
[141] Diner Out, "Across the Table", *The Table*, 23 April 1898.
[142] E. Allen Simpson, "Vegetarianism", *The Table*, 14 November 1891.
[143] "A Ball Supper Lesson at Mrs. A. B. Marshall's School of Cookery", *The Queen*, 19 May 1894.
[144] "Fancy Ices", *The Morning Post*, 20 June 1894.
[145] Agnes Bertha Marshall, *Fancy Ices,* second thousand (Robert Hayes Ltd., undated, c.1906).
[146] Because fewer copies were published, *Fancy Ices* is rarer, and therefore more expensive to buy in antiquarian bookshops than the *Book of Ices*. At the time of writing, eBay sellers are offering copies for sale at between £375 and £425.
[147] Advertisement, *The Queen*, 26 January 1895.
[148] Advertisement, *The Table*, 27 April 1895.
[149] Advertisement, *The Queen*, 7 March 1896.
[150] "Ball Supper Lesson; Marshall's Cookery Exhibition", *The Table*, 11 December 1896.
[151] "Competitions", *The Table*, 5 December 1896.
[152] "Ball Supper Lesson; Marshall's Cookery Exhibition", *The Table*, 11 December 1896.

[153] "The Queen's Hall – located in Langham Place – was the premier concert hall in pre-war London. It was the home of the BBC Symphony and the London Philharmonic Orchestras. Every year it hosted the Promenade Concerts […] On the night of 10 May 1941 the Queen's Hall was hit by a single incendiary bomb and completely gutted.", BBC – The Queen's Hall Destroyed by Bombing, accessed 15 January 2023, https://www.bbc.com/historyofthebbc/anniversaries/may/queens-hall-destroyed/.

[154] "A Ball Supper Lesson at Mrs. A. B. Marshall's", *The Queen*, 26 December 1896.

[155] *Truth*, 24 December 1896.

[156] "The Pinner Fire Brigade", *Harrow Observer*, 28 June 1895.

[157] "Pinner Parish Council Election", *Harrow Observer*, 3 April 1896.

[158] Christian Wolmar, *The Subterranean Railway* (Atlantic Books, 2012), 96.

[159] The station is now called Harrow on the Hill – Wolmar, *The Subterranean Railway*, 331 – note 6.

[160] "Mr. A. W. Marshall's Garden Party", *Harrow Observer*, 27 August 1897.

[161] This is the same Karl Kaps who had played with his Palace Orchestra at Agnes's Cookery Exhibition and Ball Supper Display in December 1896. Kaps was a composer and arranger of popular music in addition to being a band leader and musician.

[162] In England, the term "public school" refers to a private, fee-paying secondary school, not a school supported by public funds – *Oxford English Dictionary*.

[163] Michelle Higgs, *Servants' Stories* (Pen & Sword History, 2015), 12.

[164] "The Robbery at The Towers", *Harrow Observer*, 22 January 1897.

[165] "A Beautiful Present – Fancy Ices", *The Table*, 30 October 1897.
[166] "Victorian Era Exhibition, 1897", *The Table*, 6 November 1897.
[167] "Caution – Gas Cookery Exhibitions", *The Table*, 15 April 1899.
[168] Notice, *The Table*, 12 January 1901.
[169] The National Archives, BT 31/15074/31415: Company No: 31415; Table Newspaper Company Ltd. Incorporated in 1890. Dissolved between 1916 and 1932.
[170] *Ibid.*
[171] "Death and Funeral of the Late Mrs. A. B. Marshall at Pinner", *Middlesex & Buckinghamshire Advertiser*, 5 August 1905.
[172] "An Entire Dinner Lesson at Mrs. A. B. Marshall's", *The Queen*, 12 November 1904.
[173] London Metropolitan Archives, City of London, Middlesex Deeds Registry, MDR/1904/033/0751-1000, 916.
[174] A. B. Atkinson, "Wealth and Inheritance in Britain from 1896 to the Present", London School of Economics, published 12 November 2013, https://sticerd.lse.ac.uk/dps/case/cp/casepaper178.pdf, 12.
[175] "The Death of a Gifted Woman", *Cheltenham Examiner*, 2 August 1905.
[176] "Girl's Gossip", *Truth*, 17 August 1905.
[177] "The Death of a Gifted Woman", *Cheltenham Examiner*, 2 August 1905.
[178] "Memorial Window", *Uxbridge & West Drayton Gazette*, 11 August 1906.
[179] Robin Weir, John Deith, Peter Brears and Peter Barham, *Mrs Marshall: The Greatest Victorian Ice Cream Maker* (Smith Settle for Syon House, 1998), 24.

[180] "A Brief History of West End Lawn Tennis Club", Pinner West End Lawn Tennis Club, accessed 20 April 2022, https://www.pinnertennis.co.uk/brief-history-58.

[181] England & Wales Government Probate Death Index 1858–2019, Middlesex, England, 1935.

[182] "Guildford Borough Bench", *Surrey Advertiser*, 10 October 1903.

[183] The National Archives, BT 31/15074/31415: Company No: 31415; Table Newspaper Company Ltd. Incorporated in 1890. Dissolved between 1916 and 1932.

[184] "Title: The Table: a weekly paper of cookery, gastronomy, food, amusements, &c.; Contributor: A. B. Marshall (Agnes B.) Marshall's School of Cookery; Description: Vol. I, no. I (Saturday, June 12th, 1886) – Ceased in 1918", British Library, main catalogue, searched 28 March 2022.

[185] *Ibid.*

[186] "Survey of London, South-East Marylebone, Draft chapters of Volumes 51 and 52, Chapter 26: Mortimer Street", UCL – Bartlett School of Architecture, accessed 16 January 2023, https://www.ucl.ac.uk/bartlett/architecture/research/survey-london/south-east-marylebone.

[187] "High Explosive Bomb at Mortimer Street", Bomb Sight, accessed 31 May 2022, http://bombsight.org/bombs/32611/.

[188] "Books by Mrs. A.B. Marshall", *The Table*, 5 August 1905.

[189] The book is undated, but must have been published between 16 November 1912 (the date of the last advertisement that I have been able to find, and which shows earlier editions – see: Publication Dates for Agnes Marshall's Books) and 1918 when *The Table* ceased publication.

[190] "Girl's Gossip", *Truth*, 17 August 1905.

[191] Redd: tidy something up – *Oxford English Dictionary*.

[192] "The Death of a Gifted Woman", *Cheltenham Examiner*, 2 August 1905.

[193] *Ibid.*
[194] "Practical Hints on the Artificial Hatching of Pheasants' Eggs", *The Field*, 4 June 1887.
[195] "Ball Supper Lesson at Mrs. A. B. Marshall's School of Cookery", *The Queen*, 19 May 1894.
[196] Fanny Craddock, *The Sherlock Holmes Cookbook* (W. H. Allen, 1976), 7.
[197] *Ibid.*, 12.
[198] Elizabeth David, *Harvest of the Cold Months* (Michael Joseph, 1994), 63.
[199] Terry Jenkins, "The Truth about Mrs Marshall", *Petits Propos Culinaires*, 112 (Prospect Books, November 2018), 100–112.
[200] "Agnes Marshall", *Wikipedia*, accessed 8 May 2023, https://en.wikipedia.org/wiki/Agnes_Marshall.
[201] Terry Jenkins, "The Truth about Mrs Marshall", *Petits Propos Culinaires*, 112 (Prospect Books, November 2018), 103.
[202] *Ibid.*
[203] Mark Kurlansky, *Milk!: A 10,000-Year Food Fracas* (Bloomsbury Publishing, 2019), 133.
[204] Charlotte Montague, *Women of Invention: Life-Changing Ideas by Remarkable Women* (Chartwell Books, 2018), 137.
[205] "You're Dead To Me: The History of Ice Cream", BBC, accessed 23 November 2022, https://www.bbc.co.uk/programmes/articles/5cSf963VtsNDsr3qj0qCVNV/8-scoops-on-the-history-of-ice-cream.
[206] Robin Weir, John Deith, Peter Brears and Peter Barham, *Mrs Marshall: The Greatest Victorian Ice Cream Maker* (Smith Settle for Syon House, 1998), 1.
[207] "Ice Queen", *The Queen*, 19 May 1894.
[208] Mary Ellen Snodgrass, *Encyclopedia of Kitchen History* (Fitzroy Dearborn, 2004), 380.
[209] *Ibid.*, 381.

[210] "You're Dead To Me: The History of Ice Cream", BBC, accessed 23 November 2022, https://www.bbc.co.uk/programmes/articles/5cSf963VtsNDsr3qj0qCVNV/8-scoops-on-the-history-of-ice-cream.

[211] Robin Weir, John Deith, Peter Brears and Peter Barham, *Mrs Marshall: The Greatest Victorian Ice Cream Maker* (Smith Settle for Syon House, 1998), 14.

[212] Robin Weir, "Marshall [née Smith], Agnes Bertha (1855–1905)" in *Oxford Dictionary of National Biography*, Vol. 36, eds. H. G. C. Matthew and Brian Harrison, (Oxford University Press, 2004), 826.

[213] Robin Weir, John Deith, Peter Brears and Peter Barham, *Mrs Marshall: The Greatest Victorian Ice Cream Maker* (Smith Settle for Syon House, 1998), 7, 47.

[214] Diner Out, "Across the Table", *The Table*, 24 August 1901.

[215] Barham explains that "Liquified air is a mixture of around 20% liquid oxygen and 80% liquid nitrogen.", Weir *et al.*, 52.

[216] Robin Weir, John Deith, Peter Brears and Peter Barham, *Mrs Marshall: The Greatest Victorian Ice Cream Maker* (Smith Settle for Syon House, 1998), 53.

[217] Diner Out, "Across the Table", *The Table*, 23 May 1896.

[218] Diner Out, "Across the Table", *The Table*, 5 January 1901.

[219] "Taking Tea and Talking Politics: The Role of Tearooms", Historic England, accessed 29 November 2022, https://historicengland.org.uk/research/inclusive-heritage/womens-history/suffrage/taking-tea-and-talking-politics/.

[220] Robin Weir, John Deith, Peter Brears and Peter Barham, *Mrs Marshall: The Greatest Victorian Ice Cream Maker* (Smith Settle for Syon House, 1998), 2.

[221] Agnes Bertha Marshall, *Mrs. A. B. Marshall's Cookery Book,* fifteenth thousand (Simpkin, Marshall, Hamilton, Kent & Co., undated, c.1891), 329–330.

[222] Mark Kurlansky, *Milk!: A 10,000-Year Food Fracas* (Bloomsbury Publishing, 2019), 133.

[223] Agnes Bertha Marshall, *Mrs. A. B. Marshall's Cookery Book,* fifteenth thousand (Simpkin, Marshall, Hamilton, Kent & Co., undated, c.1891), 330.

[224] Charlotte Montague, *Women of Invention: Life-Changing Ideas by Remarkable Women* (Chartwell Books, 2018), 137.

[225] Ralph Pomeroy, *The Ice Cream Connection* (Paddington Press, 1975), 64.

[226] *Ibid.*, 12.

[227] Liza Picard, *Victorian London* (Phoenix, 2006), 99.

[228] Hugh McLeod, "White Collar Values and the Role of Religion" in *The Lower Middle Class in Britain 1870–1914*, ed. Geoffrey Crossick (Routledge, 2016), 61.

[229] *Ibid.*, 62.

[230] Arthur Robert Kenney-Herbert, "Wyvern", *Furlough Reminiscences* (Higginbotham & Co., 1880), 20.

[231] *Ibid.*, 19.

[232] Victoria Elizabeth Powell, "The knight from nowhere: a biographical case study of social mobility in Victorian Britain." (PhD thesis, Birkbeck University of London, 2018), 2. https://eprints.bbk.ac.uk/id/eprint/40324/1/Victoria%20Powell%20PhD.pdf.

[233] *Ibid.,* 9.

[234] Bram Stoker, *Personal Reminiscences of Henry Irving* (William Heinemann, 1906), 433.

[235] "The Death of a Gifted Woman", *Cheltenham Examiner*, 2 August 1905.

[236] Kathryn Hughes, "The middle classes: etiquette and upward mobility", British Library, published 15 May 2014, https://www.bl.uk/romantics-and-victorians/articles/the-middle-classes-etiquette-and-upward-mobility.

[237] *Ibid.*

[238] "Cookery and Cook-Making, An Interview with Mr. Marshall", *The Pall Mall Gazette*, 14 October 1886.

[239] Terry Jenkins, "The Truth about Mrs Marshall", *Petits Propos Culinaires*, 112 (Prospect Books, November 2018), 106.

[240] Kathryn Hughes, *The Short Life and Long Times of Mrs Beeton* (Harper Perennial, 2006), 4, quoting Lytton Strachey.

[241] *Ibid.*, 108.

[242] "Girl's Gossip", *Truth*, 17 August 1905.

[243] Kathryn Hughes, *The Short Life and Long Times of Mrs Beeton* (Harper Perennial, 2006), 70–72.

[244] Agnes Bertha Marshall, *Mrs. A. B. Marshall's Cookery Book,* fifteenth thousand (Simpkin, Marshall, Hamilton, Kent & Co., undated, c.1891), Preface.

[245] Kathryn Hughes, *The Short Life and Long Times of Mrs Beeton* (Harper Perennial, 2006), 189.

[246] *Ibid.*, 180.

[247] *Ibid.*, 267.

[248] *Ibid.*, 197.

[249] *Ibid.*, 198.

[250] *Ibid.*, 197–198

[251] Isabella Beeton, editor, *Beeton's Book of Household Management* (S. O. Beeton, 1861).

[252] Kathryn Hughes, *The Short Life and Long Times of Mrs Beeton* (Harper Perennial, 2006), 285.

[253] *Ibid.*, 282.

[254] Ibid., 344–345.

[255] Felicity Kinross, *Coffee and Ices: The Story of Carlo Gatti in London* (London Canal Museum, second edition, 2020), 12.
[256] *Ibid.,* 13–15.
[257] *Ibid.,* 18–19.
[258] Elizabeth David, *Harvest of the Cold Months* (Michael Joseph, 1994), 348.
[259] "Carlo Gatti: Ice Entrepreneur", London Canal Museum, accessed 21 November 2022, https://www.canalmuseum.org.uk/ice/gatti.htm.
[260] "The Ice Wells", London Canal Museum, accessed 21 November 2022, https://www.canalmuseum.org.uk/ice/ice-wells.htm.
[261] Felicity Kinross, *Coffee and Ices: The Story of Carlo Gatti in London* (London Canal Museum, second edition, 2020), 26.
[262] Margaret Visser, *Much Depends on Dinner* (McClelland and Stewart, 1987), 303.
[263] Felicity Kinross, *Coffee and Ices: The Story of Carlo Gatti in London* (London Canal Museum, second edition, 2020), 18.
[264] Henry Mayhew, *London Labour and the London Poor* (Oxford University Press, 2012), 72.
[265] Felicity Kinross, *Coffee and Ices: The Story of Carlo Gatti in London* (London Canal Museum, second edition, 2020), 15.
[266] Henry Mayhew, *London Labour and the London Poor* (Oxford University Press, 2012), 73.
[267] Gustave Doré and Blanchard Jerrold, *London: a Pilgrimage* (Grant & Co., 1872), 127.
[268] Felicity Kinross, *Coffee and Ices: The Story of Carlo Gatti in London* (London Canal Museum, second edition, 2020), 18.
[269] John Thomson and Adolphe Smith, *Street Life in London*, (Sampson Lowe, Marston, Searle, & Rivington, 1877), 53.
[270] *Ibid.,* 53.
[271] *Ibid.,* 53.

[272] *Ibid.*, 54.
[273] Street urchins – *Oxford English Dictionary*.
[274] Andrew W. Tuer, *Old London Street Cries and the Cries of Today* (Leadenhall Press, 1885), 58.
[275] Felicity Kinross, *Coffee and Ices: The Story of Carlo Gatti in London* (London Canal Museum, second edition, 2020), 18.
[276] Margaret Visser, *Much Depends on Dinner* (McClelland and Stewart, 1987), 303.
[277] Andrew W. Tuer, *Old London Street Cries and the Cries of Today* (Leadenhall Press, 1885), 58–60.
[278] Margaret Visser, *Much Depends on Dinner* (McClelland and Stewart, 1987), 303.
[279] Robin Weir, "Penny Licks and Hokey Pokey, Ice Cream Before the Cone", in *Oxford Symposium on Food and Cookery 1991: Public Eating*, ed. Harlan Walker (Prospect Books, 1991), 296.
[280] *Ibid.*, 297.
[281] *Ibid.*, 298–299.
[282] George Paddock Bate, M.D., *Report on the sanitary condition and vital statistics of the Parish of St. Matthew, Bethnal Green during the year 1895* (Printed by J. Williams-Cook, 1896), 28. Accessed via "London's Pulse: Medical Officer of Health reports 1848–1972", Wellcome Library, https://wellcomelibrary.org/moh/report/b17997719/28#?m=0&cv=29&c=0&s=0&z=-0.3754%2C0.7515%2C2.0078%2C0.7838.
[283] Medical Officer of Health, *Annual Report of the Medical Officer of Health of the Administrative County of London 1898* (London County Council, 1898), 9. Accessed via "London's Pulse: Medical Officer of Health reports 1848–1972", Wellcome Library, https://wellcomelibrary.org/moh/report/b18252473/142#?m=0

&cv=142&c=0&s=0&z=-0.0226%2C0.1346%2C1.2619%2C0.4926.

[284] Felicity Kinross, *Coffee and Ices: The Story of Carlo Gatti in London* (London Canal Museum, second edition, 2020), 27.

[285] Diner Out, "Across The Table", *The Table*, 25 August 1900.

[286] Agnes Bertha Marshall, *Fancy Ices,* second thousand (Robert Hayes Ltd., undated, c.1906), Introduction.

[287] "Torpedo Ice", *Norfolk News*, 22 March 1884.

[288] Agnes Bertha Marshall, *Fancy Ices,* second thousand (Robert Hayes Ltd., undated, c.1906), 94–95.

[289] "Torpedo Ice", *Norfolk News*, 22 March 1884.

[290] Hugh McLeod, "White Collar Values and the Role of Religion" in *The Lower Middle Class in Britain 1870–1914*, ed. Geoffrey Crossick (Routledge, 2016), 63.

[291] "Amara Veritas", *The Servant Problem: An Attempt at Its Solution by an Experienced Mistress* (Simpkin, Marshall, Hamilton, Kent & Co. 1899), 6–7.

[292] *Ibid.*, 7.

[293] Ibid., 5–6.

[294] Arthur Robert Kenney-Herbert, "Wyvern", "Etcætera from Town", *The Athenaeum and Daily News*, 1 October 1877.

[295] "Amara Veritas", *The Servant Problem: An Attempt at Its Solution by an Experienced Mistress* (Simpkin, Marshall, Hamilton, Kent & Co. 1899), 121.

[296] Michelle Higgs, *Servants' Stories* (Pen & Sword History, 2015), 49.

[297] *Ibid.*, 45.

[298] "Amara Veritas", *The Servant Problem: An Attempt at Its Solution by an Experienced Mistress* (Simpkin, Marshall, Hamilton, Kent & Co. 1899), 22.

[299] Arthur Robert Kenney-Herbert, "Wyvern", "Etcætera from Town", *The Athenaeum and Daily News*, 1 October 1877.

[300] "Amara Veritas", *The Servant Problem: An Attempt at Its Solution by an Experienced Mistress* (Simpkin, Marshall, Hamilton, Kent & Co. 1899), 35.
[301] "The Great Servant Question", *The Table*, 2 October 1886.
[302] Arthur Robert Kenney-Herbert, "The Teaching of Cookery", *The Nineteenth Century*, May 1906.
[303] Calculation made using the Bank of England Inflation Calculator, accessed 9 January 2023, https://www.bankofengland.co.uk/monetary-policy/inflation/inflation-calculator.
[304] Dorothy Stone, *The National: The Story of a Pioneer College* (Robert Hale & Company, 1976), 8.
[305] Eliza Youmans, quoted in: Dorothy Stone, *The National: The Story of a Pioneer College* (Robert Hale & Company, 1976), 26.
[306] "Table Talk", *The Table*, 3 March 1888.
[307] Advertisements for Marshall's School of Cookery, National Training School of Cookery and Common-Sense Cookery Association, *The Morning Post*, 27 October 1894.

Index

A

Across the Table, 65, 66, 95
Acton, Eliza, 106, 108
Amara Veritas, 122, 124, 125, 126, 127

B

Ball Supper Lesson, 63, 64, 67, 68, 70, 75, 86
  photograph, 64
  review, 64, 65, 71
  ticket sales, 63
Barham, Peter, 7, 88, 94
BBC article, 92, 93, 94
Bedford Lemere, 64
Beeton, Isabella, 85, 104, 106, 107, 108
Beeton, Samuel, 105, 106, 108
Beeton's Book of Household Management, 76, 106, 107, 108
Book of Ices
  copies published, 68, 69, 75, 76, 84
  published, 21
  recipes, 23

Booth, Charles, 11, 16
Box, William W., 53, 79
Brears, Peter, 7, 88
Brillat-Savarin, 45
British class system, 98
British Orphan Asylum, 12
Buckmaster, John Charles, 129

C

Cabinet Refrigerator, 28
Carême, Antonin, 45
Cavendish Rooms, 63, 64
Chilton, Messrs., 63
Clarke, Mrs Charles, 130
Cole, Sir Henry, 128, 129
Common-Sense Cookery Association, 127, 131
Cookery Book
  contents, 42
  copies published, 50, 58, 69, 75, 76, 84
  published, 41
  revised and enlarged edition, 69
  sample menu, 43
Cookery Exhibition and Ball Supper Display, 70

cookery lesson - the most important ever given, 63
Cowan's Baking Powder, 69, 70, 75
Craddock, Fanny, 7, 87
Crusoe, Edwin Adolphus Ross, 13

D

David, Elizabeth, 88
Deith, John, 7, 9, 14, 56, 88, 89, 94
dessert - Victorian meaning of, 46
Diner Out, 65, 66, 67, 95
Doré, Gustave, 113
Dowgate Bonded Warehouse, 13
dressed vegetables, 47

E

Eagle Range and Foundry Company, 70
Entire Dinner Lesson, 28, 35, 36, 61, 63, 75, 76, 79
reviews, 35
Exposition Culinaire Internationale, 20

F

Fancy Ices, 67, 68, 92, 120
chapters, 67
copies published, 68, 76, 84
Francatelli, Charles Elmé, 85
Fry, J. S. & Sons (chocolate), 70

G

Gatti, Agostino, 119
Gatti, Carlo, 97, 110, 111, 112, 113, 114, 119
Gatti, Stephano, 119
gentleman - Victorian usage of term, 98
Golders Green Crematorium, 78, 82
Gunter's, 119

H

Hamwi, Ernest, 96
Hansard Publishing Union, 51
Higgs, Michelle, 8, 124
hokey pokey ice cream, 117
hokey pokey men, 116
Houghton, William, 13
Hovis bread, 71
Hughes, Kathryn, 100, 104

I

Ice Cave, 21, 28, 34
   patent granted, 19
International and Colonial Congress on Inebriety, 37
International Food and Cookery Exhibition, 20
International Inventions Exhibition, 20
Irving, Henry, 100, 102

J

Jenkins, Terry, 9, 10, 11, 57, 89, 90, 91, 102
Jerrold, Blanchard, 113
Johnson, Nancy, 19

K

Kaps, Karl, 71, 73
Kenney-Herbert, Colonel Arthur, 7, 99, 123, 127, 128, 129
Kinross, Felicity, 110, 112, 113
Kurlansky, Mark, 92, 96

L

lady - Victorian usage of term, 31, 98
Larger Cookery Book
   contents, 59
   copies published, 69, 75, 76, 78, 84
   illustrations, 60
   published, 58
   reviews, 60
Lavenue School of Cookery, 16, 17, 32, 93, 102
Liebig's Extract of Meat Company, 70, 76
London Canal Museum, 111
London Labour and the London Poor, 112
London: a Pilgrimage, 113
Luxette, 68, 75

M

Mappin and Webb, 63
Maps Descriptive of London Poverty, 11
Marquis, Monsieur, 71
Married Women's Property Act, 57
Marshall, Agnes Alfreda, 13, 14, 15, 56, 77, 82
Marshall, Agnes Bertha
   accident, 76

appearance, 84
as editor of *The Table*, 25, 65
as single mother, 15
born as Agnes Beere Smith, 10, 89, 90
born as Agnes Bertha Smith, 11
buys The Towers, 56
carriage accident, 50
ceases to be editor of *The Table*, 37
charity dinners, 39, 48, 49
cremation and burial, 78
dies, 78
doubts over year of birth, 9, 11, 77, 89
early life, 9
gift of locket, 27, 85
gifts The Towers to Alfred, 79
ice cream cornets, 96
increases shareholding in The Table, 55
known as Queen of Ices, 92
lack of obituary in *The Table*, 80
later years, 85
launches cookery school, 16
launches *The Table*, 25
lecture tour of USA, 48
marries Alfred William Marshall, 11, 101
memorial service, 81
memorial window, 10, 81
obituaries, 80, 81
provincial tour, 33, 48
studies cookery in Paris and Vienna, 12, 102
using liquid nitrogen to make ice cream, 94, 96

Marshall, Alfred Harold, 15, 56, 77, 79, 82

Marshall, Alfred William, 73, 95
as gelatine merchant, 82
as wine merchant, 12, 13, 49
early life, 12
elected county councillor, 72
employed at Oakley House Gentleman's School, 12
employed at Stationers' School, 14
fiftieth birthday party, 73
gifted The Towers by Agnes, 79
marries Agnes Bertha Smith, 11
marries Gertrude Mary Walsh, 81
President of Pinner Fire Brigade, 72
sentenced at Old Bailey, 12

Marshall, Ethel, 15, 56
born as Ethel Smith, 15, 91
marriage, 77

Marshall, Rosalie Osborn, 82

Marshall, William Edward, 15, 56, 77, 82, 83
Marshall's products, 61
   Coralline Pepper, 75
   Cowan's Baking Powder, 69
   culinary moulds, 28
   curry powder, 48
   food colouring, 48
   fruit syrups, 28
   gelatine, 28, 35, 48
   Luxette, 68
   Sildeen Consommé, 75
   Silver Rays White Rum, 75
   slicer, 49
   wines and spirits, 49
Marshall's School of Cookery
   acquires 32 Mortimer Street, 27
   advertisements, 17, 27, 131
   Agnes's method of teaching, 30
   buys Lavenue School of Cookery, 16
   ceases trading, 83
   dispute with rival school, 32
   expands warehouses, 27
   fees, 29
   John Osborn Wells as manager, 77
   moves to 30 Mortimer Street, 16
   new classroom, 27
   non-payment of fess, 18
   opening months, 17
   programme, 28
   pupil numbers, 24
Marshall's services, 62
Masters, Thomas, 19, 24
Mayhew, Henry, 112
McLeod, Hugh, 98, 122
Metropolitan Railway, 72
middle class, 16, 22, 39, 87, 89, 91, 98, 99, 101, 105, 107, 113, 120, 122, 131
Middlesex Deeds Register, 56
Montague, Charlotte, 92, 97
Mrs Beeton. *See* Beeton, Isabella
Mrs Marshall: The Greatest Victorian Ice Cream Maker, 9, 14, 88, 89, 92, 93, 94, 96

N

National Training School of Cookery, 32, 92, 93, 128, 129, 130, 131
   criticised by Agnes, 33, 131

O

Old London Street Cries, 115
Olde Cheshire Cheese, 96
Osler, F. & C., 63

Oxford Dictionary of National Biography, 94

P

Paris Exhibition, 50
Patent Freezer, 19, 20, 23, 28, 34
   patent granted, 19
patents granted to women, 19
penny licks, 115
   as health hazard, 117
   Medical Officer of Health report, 118
Picard, Liza, 98
Pinner Cemetery, 78, 82
Pinner Parish Church, 10, 81
Piper & Son, 71
Pomeroy, Ralph, 97
Powell, Victoria, 99, 102
Pretty Luncheon, 9, 33, 37, 38, 39, 47
   menu, 34
   reviews, 38
Princess Christian, 49, 58, 100, 103

Q

Queen Victoria, 49, 64, 85, 100, 104, 129

Queen's Hall, 71

R

Richardson, Ruth, 15
Royal Adelaide Gallery, 119
Ruffin, Napoleon, 52, 53, 64
Rugby School, 73

S

Senn, C. Herman, 76
service à la Française, 44
service à la Russe, 45
Sherlock Holmes Cookbook, 7, 87
Smith, Adolphe, 114
Smith, John, 9, 10, 89, 101
Smith, Sarah, 90
Smith, Susan, 9, 10, 89, 90, 91, 101
Snodgrass, Mary Ellen, 92, 93
Spottiswoode & Co., 51
Stone, Dorothy, 129
Street Life in London, 114

T

Table Newspaper Company Limited
   change in shareholding, 55, 78, 83

company officers, 53
directors, 77
incorpoartion, 51
moves registered offices, 54
shareholders, 52
voluntary liquidation, 83
William Edward Marshall as director, 83
Table Talk, 25, 54, 65, 66
Table, The, 8
annual, 31, 39
change in content, 54
change of format, 65
changes June 1887, 36
changes October 1891, 54
closes, 83
dispute with publishers, 51
editor, 25
incorporated as limited company, 51
launched, 25
readership, 26
reduction in price, 53
subscriptions, 26, 53
Tempting Repast, 49, 62
Thomson, John, 114
Thomson, Raphael, 22
Torpedo Ice, 120
Towers, The, 57, 72, 77
Agnes buys the property, 56
Agnes dies at, 78, 93
Agnes transfers ownership to Alfred, 79
Alfred and Gertrude living at, 82
death of workman at, 58
fire brigades rally at, 72
theft at, 74
Tuer, Andrew, 115

U

upper class, 98
upper ten, 60, 103

V

vegetarian movement, 66
Victorian Era Exhibition, 75
Visser, Margaret, 112, 116

W

Walsh, Gertrude Mary, 81
Ward Lock, 84, 108
Weir, Robin, 7, 19, 88, 92, 94, 116
Wells, Ada Martha, 56, 77
formerly Ada Martha Wells Smith, 11
Wells, Charles, 10
Wells, John Osborn, 51, 53, 54, 55, 56, 77
formerly John Osborn Wells Smith, 11
manager of Marshall's School of Cookery, 77

Wells, John senior, 10, 11, 89, 90, 101
Wells, Mary Sarah
   formerly Mary Sarah Wells Smith, 11, 90
West End Lawn Tennis Club, 82

Wilde, Oscar, 41
Willis's Rooms, 9, 37, 38, 39
Woman's World, 41
working class, 98, 101, 102, 104, 112, 113, 125, 131

Printed in Great Britain
by Amazon